HANDY
PET CARE
GUIDES

Choosing &
Looking After Your

Dog

This is a **FLAME TREE** book
First published in 2014

Publisher and Creative Director: Nick Wells
Senior Project Editor: Catherine Taylor
Picture Research: Victoria Lyle, Gemma Walters
Art Director: Mike Spender
Layout Design: Jane Ashley
Copy Editor: Emily Anderson
Indexer: Eileen Cox

Special thanks to: Esme Chapman, Emma Chafer, Naomi Waters, Ellie Bowden, Helen Tovey and Sara Robson

FLAME TREE PUBLISHING
Crabtree Hall, Crabtree Lane
Fulham, London SW6 6TY
United Kingdom

www.flametreepublishing.com

First published 2014

16 18 17 15
3 5 7 9 10 8 6 4

Every effort has been made to contact copyright holders. We apologize in advance for any omissions and would be pleased to insert the appropriate acknowledgement in subsequent editions of this publication.

A CIP record for this book is available from the British Library upon request.

ISBN 978-1-78361-230-7

Printed in China

Picture Credits:
Ardea: John Daniels 131. **Carol Ann Johnson**: 79, 81, 164, 168, 193, 198, 228, 237. **Corbis**: Bettmann 15, 69; Bohemian Nomad Picturemakers 14, 241; Carlos Carrion 16; Darren Staples/Reuters 19; David Michael Zimmerman 22; DLILLC 33; Dung Vo Trung 37; Elder Neville 40; Heiko Wolfraum 41; Historical Picture Archive 42; Hulton-Deutsch Collection 62; Kay Nietfeld/epa 63; LWA-Dann Tardif 68, 89, 91, 93; Nir Elias 88; Paper Rodeo 90; Paul Hilton/epa 128; Peter Dench 149; PoodlesRock 160, 161; Ricardo Azoury 185; Rob Howard 205; Stapleton Collection 219; Tom Nebbia 220; Corbis 236. **DK Images**: 146, 147, 148, 172, 186, 189, 192, 206, 209, 210, 211, 216, 217, 224, 234, 235, 243. **FLPA**: Angela Hampton 4, 117; David Dalton 28, 49, 94–95, 116bl, 118, 121, 126, 127, 129, 132, 133, 134, 135, 136, 151, 153; David Hosking 32, 52; David T. Grewcock 35; Dirk Enters 46; Foto Natura Catalogue 47, 50; Gerard Lacz 53, 57; Mark Raycroft 110; Mitsuaki Iwago 120; Phil McLean 125; Roger Tidman 141; Simon Hosking 195; Stefanie Krause-Wieczorek 214; Wayne Hutchinson 232. **Foundry Arts**: 97, 99, 101, 102, 103, 104, 105, 107, 109, 111, 112. **iStock**: 176. **Kennel Club Picture Library**: 1, 17, 23, 30, 31, 34, 39, 44, 48, 54, 55, 59, 61, 77, 108, 143, 159, 169, 184, 191, 212. **Mary Evans Picture Library**: 13, 65. **Shutterstock**: Grace Victoria 1br, 130; Eric Isselée 3br, 38, 122; Robynrg 3c, 4tl, 165; Emmanuelle Bonzami 5br, 76, 157, 213; Phil Date 5tr, 154–5, 179; Dee Hunter 7, 188; ChameleonsEye 11; Helga Esteb 12; Lavaria Ferreri Liotti 20; Regien Paassen 21; Dora Zett 24; Waldemar Dabrowski 26; Yuri Arcurs 27; Tina Rencelj 29; TheSupe87 36; Tan Kian Khoon 45; Iztok Noc 51; Jerri Adams 56; Ivonne Wierink 58; Lee319 64; plastique 70; Sebastien Gauthier 71; Gualberto Becerra 72; Damien Richard 73; Tomas Hlavacek 74; K. Kolygo 75; Laura Aqui 78; Rick's Photography 80; clearviewstock 82; pixshots 83, 187; Stephen Coburn 85, 158; Joe Gough 86; Natalia V Guesva 87; Joy Miller 100 ; jadimages 106; Muh 113; Ana de Sousa 114; Utekhina Anna 115, 123; IgorXIII 119; Maxim Petrichuk 124; Stanimir G.Stoev 138; Jeffrey Ong Guo Xiong 139; foaloce 140; Jack Gau 145; Jan Erasmus 150; Julie DeGuia 162; Wendy Kaveney Photography 163; WilleeCole 166; Jean Frooms167; HANA 170; Martin Garnham 171; Joy Brown 173, 180–1; f8grapher 174; Andresr 175; In-Finity 177; Tootles 178; Paul Clarke 183; Elliot Westacott 190; Crystal Kirk 194; Justin Kinney 196; Arvind Balaraman 197; Brberrys 199; Ursula 201; Monika Wisniewska 203; Marek Pawluczuk 207 ; Nikolai Tsvetkov 215; Emilia Kun 221; Shutterstock 223; afarland 225; Temelko Temelkov 227; Pieter 231; Andraz Cerar 233; Lori Carpenter 239; Patricia Marroquin 247. **Superstock**: Iberfoto 25; Superstock 66. **TopFoto**: 43, 67, 137, 144.

HANDY PET CARE GUIDES

Choosing & Looking After Your

Dog

SEAN O'MEARA & MICHAEL HAYWARD

**FLAME TREE
PUBLISHING**

Contents

Introduction

There's no better companionship than that of a dog. Whether it is the heart-warming affection given after a long winter walk or the comforting reassurance in times of trauma – dogs will always offer loyalty in return for a loving home. This guide offers a comprehensive selection of detailed information that showcases why a dog is truly a man's best friend.

With practical information on preparing and caring for your dog, *Choosing & Looking After Your Dog* is a great resource for those considering getting their first dog as well as more experienced dog owners. The book contains useful information on how to prepare for the arrival of a new dog, how to provide the best nutrition and what to do in a medical emergency. Every aspect of pet dog ownership is covered, from taking care of and training puppies to details on how to accommodate an older dog and even breeding and showing.

Detailed diagrams and in-depth descriptions of the anatomy, senses and abilities of the dog will allow the reader to know their animal from head to paw. Canine instinct and behaviour will be brought to life as the book guides you through the many, varying aspects of a dog's psychological make-up including intelligence and personality types.

Choosing & Looking After Your Dog is an indispensable guide for all dog lovers – from those experiencing the joy of bringing home their first dog to those who are seasoned owners – there is something for everyone.

For the Love of
Dogs

A Creature of Many Roles

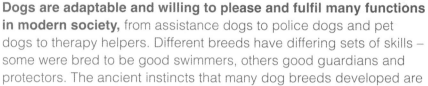

Dogs are adaptable and willing to please and fulfil many functions in modern society, from assistance dogs to police dogs and pet dogs to therapy helpers. Different breeds have differing sets of skills – some were bred to be good swimmers, others good guardians and protectors. The ancient instincts that many dog breeds developed are still useful today: herding dogs make excellent watchdogs, while scent hounds and the gun-dog breeds make invaluable scent-detection dogs. The domestic canine truly has developed to become an animal with many varied talents.

Dogs at War

Throughout history dogs have laid down their lives for us. Which is why without the help of man's best friend the history of warfare would be very different. In fact, every war since the formation of the Persian Empire in 550 BC has featured dogs. From the Roman conquests to the modern and high-tech wars of today, dogs have played many important roles – carrying supplies, finding injured soldiers and even going behind enemy lines.

Whether they were sniffing out weapons in Iraq like Buster the Springer Spaniel from England, or warning their masters of impending attack, as Bandit the German Shepherd did in Vietnam, dogs are invaluable to man during conflict. Attila the Hun, Frederick the Great and Adolph Hitler all had dogs specially trained for war.

Certain breeds only exist today because of their usefulness during conflict. With their diverse range of skills and their unrivalled courage, dogs are often the difference between victory and defeat when used in warfare.

How Dogs Conquered the Americas

When the Spanish conquistadors invaded the Americas in 1492 they did not realize what a battle they were about to face. The natives were prepared to fight to protect their land and the Spanish invaders were often outnumbered. One of the advantages the army of invaders had over those whom they were attempting to colonize was the help of their dogs.

The invaders brought with them an ancient breed of dog, similar to the Bloodhound of today. However, these were no pet dogs – they were four-legged warriors, trained to hunt down and catch escaping natives on command. The dogs were lean, strong and primed for battle, and without them it is doubtful that the outnumbered and tired invaders would have succeeded in conquering the Americas.

From The Western Front to Hollywood

Rin Tin Tin is one of the most loved and remembered of canine film stars. 'Rinty', as his fans knew him, had his own radio series, numerous film accolades and a very healthy income. But life could have been so different for this plucky German Shepherd. During routine procedures

◀ Rin Tin Tin, the famous canine film star on the Hollywood red carpet in 2011.

▶ Serving with the Red Cross in 1915, this disciplined dog tracks down a wounded German soldier.

on the Western Front in the final stages of the First World War, an American serviceman named Lee Duncan found a shell-shocked and scared little pup cowering in a bombed-out shelter in Northern France. The American took the dog back to America after the war, trained him to do some tricks and the rest is history.

Specially Trained Dogs Defeat the Nazis

Many historians credit the harsh Russian winters for helping the Allies to defeat the Nazis in the Second World War. Hitler's armies could not penetrate the frozen terrain to reach the Russian forces. But if the weather was keeping the Nazis from reaching the Russians, how did the Russians reach the Nazis? The answer was that the Red Army had more than 50,000 dogs, enabling soldiers who were lost or injured to be rescued and ensuring that the hostile conditions did not radically deplete their numbers as they marched towards Germany.

A German Helping the Allies

During one battle near the town of Duminichi in Russia, a German Shepherd named Bob managed to find 16 men hiding in the trenches. Bob lay down beside the wounded men, offering warmth, while the soldiers used the medical supplies that he was carrying around his neck. During the course of the war Russian sled dogs carried more than 1,000 injured men to safety and transported more than 300 tonnes of ammunition.

◄ Hitler playing with a young German Shepherd dog, 1940s. Famed for their loyalty, dogs have been trained by many military leaders.

► A scraggy stray 'guarding' a napping American Marine, Palau Islands, 1944: the bond between man and dog is deep and mutual.

Dogs in Sport

Dogs have played a big part in many sporting and leisure pursuits throughout their domestication. Some are proudly remembered and even continued today, while others were cruel and barbaric and every effort is made to keep those practices confined to history. The dog has many attributes that man has endeavoured to improve on – scenting, hunting, running and even guarding – and there is much competition in developing these canine skills. Whether performing alone or competing alongside us, sporting dogs represent a proud tradition.

Racing

Sight hounds, such as the Greyhound and the Whippet, are bred for speed and stamina. Their lean, lithe physiques made them inescapable pursuers on the plains of Africa, where they were initially

bred to chase and catch big game, and in the now-banned sport of hare coursing in the UK. Nowadays racing is a very popular spectator sport; Greyhound racing in particular attracts large crowds and is a popular sport on which to gamble. The dogs instinctively are driven to chase when they see fast movement, hence the name 'sight hound'. It is not necessary, therefore, to train a hound how to race, but professional racing-dog owners do put a lot of effort and planning into diet and fitness programmes. Sadly, there are concerns over the welfare of dogs used for racing. A dog's racing retirement age is around four or five years old; after that they are of no use to the trainer and, in some cases, they are neglected or killed.

Dog Fighting

Thankfully dog fighting is mostly a thing of the past, although sadly it still goes on in certain parts of the world. Many breeds of dog, such as the American Pit Bull Terrier and the Tosa Inu (or Japanese Tosa), were bred specifically for their tenacity and strength, and when these attributes were historically of use to us – for hunting and guarding for example – it was common for dogs to be pitted against each other. The owner of the winning dog could expect to be rewarded with money, prestige and fame. Dog fighting has been outlawed in most parts of the world for a long time, and many of the breeds used for the pursuit have now become popular pets.

Baiting

In some cultures badger and bear baiting were once popular 'blood sports'. In England during the nineteenth century bear baiting attracted large and enthusiastic audiences. Large, strong dogs would be set upon the bears who, typically, were impeded in some way – often having their claws removed so that they could not injure the dogs. The bloody outcome was usually defeat for the bear, as when one dog became injured or tired more would be sent into the pit. Fortunately

◄ The Japanese Tosa, shown, and the Pit Bull Terrier were both bred to encourage aggressive behaviour for dog fights.

► Dogs were not only encouraged to fight one another; another vicious sport devised by man and involving dogs was badger baiting.

bear baiting is extremely rare nowadays and rightly is considered barbaric.

Agility

When dogs compete in any sport they are displaying their natural abilities as a breed. Any natural ability that a dog possesses is of use to man, which is why there has been a tradition of people wishing to demonstrate the prowess of their dog. Today, canine agility is a popular sport where dogs compete against each other.

Assault courses containing jumps, see-saws, hoops and other obstacles are the principal way to test a dog's agility. Herding breeds, such as the Border Collie and the German Shepherd, are naturally agile and thrive in the agility arena. Special training is required to equip the dog with the obedience and understanding required to compete at agility. Agility is a popular feature at The Westminster Dog Show, Crufts and many other international canine events.

◄ Assault courses for dogs contain various obstacles including slalom poles.

► The Border Collie is a naturally agile breed and often performs well on assault courses.

Dogs and Travel

Before mechanization and the Industrial Revolution, dogs did many of the jobs that are now performed by machine. Prior to the invention of motor cars, dogs were essential to many people for travel. With many dog breeds possessing great strength, they have proven themselves as invaluable travel companions over the years. Even today, certain cultures and communities rely on dogs to get them about. There are even specific breeds of dog that were developed to help man get from place to place.

▲ With a keen pack instinct, great strength and stamina, the skills of the Husky provide vital transport for the Inuit people.

Sled Dogs

Pound for pound, the Husky is one of the strongest animals on Earth, with an impressive amount of weight-shifting strength, enduring stamina and sheer will to 'mush'. Without the Husky and other sled-dog breeds life would be decidedly difficult for the Inuit people of Alaska and Canada.

All sled dogs have a high pack-drive, which means they are self-governing. There is always an alpha that leads the pack and the other dogs then fall into line behind the lead dog. The Alaskan Malamute is a popular pet in Europe and America, but it still possesses strong pack instincts. To look at and touch a sled dog breed is to appreciate their impressive pulling and running abilities.

Carriage Dogs

The distinguished Dalmatian was initially bred to be a carriage dog. The dog's role was to run alongside carriages and chariots occupied by noble men and women. With strong guarding instincts, the Dalmatian was favoured for its protectiveness over the occupants of the carriage. For this reason Dalmatians are often associated with royalty and nobility, but in reality they are inextricably linked to ancient travellers, such as the Roma or Romany Gypsies.

Today the Dalmatian is a popular pet, but the breed still retains many of the qualities that first made it popular. Many trainers claim that the Dalmatian is a difficult dog to teach due to its independent and inquisitive streak, but the truth is that its intelligence and confidence when properly harnessed make it an excellent working or family dog.

Guardian Dogs

Many guardian breeds were developed to protect property and others were used to protect those who had to travel, such as traders. The Rottweiler, now popular for its confident and friendly temperament, was originally bred to accompany merchants in Germany. Before refrigeration butchers had to get their meat to their customers quickly, but they also faced the threat of robbery from highwaymen. In the town of Rottweil in Germany, which was a

◄ The Dalmatian is an intelligent and confident breed, and was initially bred as a carriage dog.

► Carriage dogs guarded their noble owners whilst travelling.

trading centre, a group of notable residents bred a strong, courageous dog to protect those delivering meat.

Another German breed, the Doberman, was bred by a tax collector named Louis Dobermann. Dobermann was always being attacked due to his job so he bred Manchester Terriers with German Shepherds and Rottweilers to produce a formidable travelling guard dog.

Seafaring Dogs

Many breeds became popular among sailors, fishermen and pirates due to their swimming, retrieving and companionship attributes. The Portuguese Water Dog, with its thick, waterproof

coat, was employed to bring in the nets when fishing boats went ashore. The Newfoundland, a large and strong breed with exceptional swimming abilities, accompanied sailors on their journeys as a canine lifeguard. If a man went overboard the Newfoundland would be commanded to enter the ice-cold sea (kept warm by his thick coat) to bring the man back to the boat. The Coton De Tulear was popular among pirates and sea merchants as a lap dog. The breed is one of the best-travelled in history, having been established in many parts of the world for centuries.

◄ Physically strong, Rottweilers were bred by merchants from the German town of Rottweil to protect their valuable meat trade.

► Like postmen, tax collector Louis Dobermann was frequently attacked, so bred the optimum guard dog, the Doberman.

Dogs as Pets and Helpers

The concept of dogs as house pets is a relatively new one. Man domesticated the wolf 15,000 years ago to assist his own evolution: every dog had a job. Due to technological innovations many dog breeds are now redundant, but over the course of their relationship man and dog have forged strong bonds. The dog's loyalty and intelligence have made canine companionship a desirable commodity for the human race. And as our needs change we find new and complex jobs for dogs to do for us.

Pet Dogs

Labrador Retrievers, German Shepherds and Boxers are among the most popular pet breeds in the world. The first people to keep dogs as companion animals rather than working dogs are thought to have been Chinese Emperors. Small breeds such as the Shih Tzu were favoured for their size and personality, often displaying great devotion and loyalty to one person above all others.

Today people choose pet dogs for many different reasons. Some people like their dogs to match their own personality, while other people choose dogs that will fit in well with their lifestyle or home environment. Many of the attributes that made certain breeds popular for working are now reasons for their popularity as pets. Conversely, some dogs have seen their original working attributes bred out to accommodate them as pets. Many present-day dog breeds are comparable to their working ancestors in appearance only.

Pet Dogs That Work

Some dogs that are kept as pets may still be used for a combination of work and companionship. Many retriever breeds, such as the Labrador Retriever and the Springer Spaniel are popular choices for pets but are used frequently for assistance in leisure pursuits, such as hunting and shooting. Often people who hunt or shoot find that keeping their working dog as a pet enables them to forge a closer and more co-operative relationship with their dog.

Herding dogs are often kept as pets too, particularly dogs that are put to work on farms. In many cases a working dog may retire due to old age or ill health and will simply make the transition from working companion to pet.

Assistance Dogs as Pets

Due to the domestic nature of their work, most assistance dogs are kept as pets. Guide dogs are required to assist their blind owners at all times and therefore need to be present throughout the day and night. To facilitate this it is necessary that the dog fulfil the role of pet and working dog simultaneously. This is normally the preferable arrangement, as the dog benefits from the company and interaction with

◄ Chinese Emperors, who favoured Shih Tzus, are often thought to be the first people to own dogs simply for their companionship.

► Companion or colleague, several breeds of dog, such as Labrador Retrievers or Springer Spaniels, make both excellent pets and working dogs.

the owner and becomes familiar with their needs and requirements in terms of assistance. Pastoral and retriever breeds are popular choices as assistance dogs due to their high intelligence and biddable nature.

The Many Types of Assistance Dog

Dogs are bred and trained to help humans in many different situations. People with disabilities are often the beneficiaries of canine help. Dogs have been trained successfully to serve as guide dogs for blind people, hearing dogs for deaf people and as epilepsy-seizure-alert dogs. Sometimes people requiring the assistance of a dog will receive a companion that is trained to suit their unique needs. People using wheelchairs and people with limited mobility are given specially trained assistance dogs that can perform roles as diverse as using cash machines, picking up items from shop shelves, answering the door and even, in the case of one Labrador Retriever from England, putting their owner into the recovery position.

► Dogs are used to assist people with many disabilities. Here a boy with cerebal palsy enjoys the company of his assistant.

Search and Rescue Dogs

One of the few things that dogs can do better than any machine is detect scent. Some dogs can even track scent across running water. This is why dogs are still put to good use in search-and-rescue situations. A combination of agility, scenting ability and intelligence means that dogs remain the ultimate tool in finding missing or injured persons.

Dogs and Natural Disasters

Search and rescue in natural-disaster situations requires dogs that are calm and intelligent. All dogs have a strong sense of smell so the most sophisticated canine nose is not always necessary – it is often more important for the dog to be agile and intelligent so that it can be commanded to perform very specific functions. In earthquake situations Springer Spaniels are often seen searching collapsed buildings to find people who are trapped. Dogs can differentiate between survivors and people who have died, which means, in extreme situations, their handlers can prioritize.

◄   Legendary mountain rescue dog the St Bernard can keep a person warm in harsh high-altitude conditions.

►   The keen scent of smell of the Springer Spaniel can track a scent across running water; a great search and rescue aid.

Hostile Environments

Cold countries are often home to excellent tracking dogs. This is due to the environmental factors that were at play when breeds were being developed. The St Bernard is one of the most popular breeds used in mountain rescue. The dog needs to have a keen sense of smell as well as the ability to help a person to remain warm. This is achieved by training the dog to lie with a victim once they are located. There are many search-and-rescue methods used that involve dogs. Sometimes dogs are required simply to signal the location of a person in need of help, while at other times it is necessary for them to move the victim by pulling them out.

Gun Dogs and Sporting Dogs

Retriever breeds such as Springer and Cocker Spaniels are frequently used to locate people trapped and injured in natural disasters. Specially trained for the job, these dogs need to be the most intelligent, obedient and calm-natured. Due to their instinct to find and retrieve, these dogs are very effective at locating a scent. Large dogs are often unsuitable for this sort of work, which often rules out scent hounds.

Scent Hounds

Bloodhounds, Beagles and Basset Hounds are all popular search-and-rescue breeds and many people owe their lives to the highly sensitive noses of these

◄ Scent hounds often have large ears to help trap scent near the muzzle, enabling them to track even the faintest scent.

► A German Shepherd in training for the Fire Service, to help firemen to search collapsed buildings and landslides for missing people.

dogs. The power of the canine sense of smell is frequently underestimated, and scent hounds are the best of all types of dog at tracking a scent.

Originally bred to track prey using the sense of smell, all scent hounds are in possession of highly sophisticated and large scent receptors. Look at a scent hound and you will notice it has large ears and a wrinkly face. This is to enable the dog to perform better scent detection, as the large ears shield a scent source from the wind and the folds in the face trap scent near to the nose. Scent hounds are important in cases where people are mobile – an escaped prisoner for example. In these situations the dog needs to be able to track a moving scent rather than a static one, so this work can only be done by dogs with the strongest sense of smell.

Pastoral and Herding Breeds

Breeds used for herding, such as Border Collies, Briards and German Shepherds are effective in search-and-rescue situations due to their high intelligence and tenacity. Many police forces favour these breeds, and they are often the first dogs on the scene at any situation requiring search and rescue.

► Briards, as well as Border Collies and German Shepherds, are intelligent and tenacious, willing to keep searching for victims in need of rescue.

Police and Tracking Dogs

Dogs possess a phenomenal array of different skills, so from guarding to scent detection police forces around the world have found numerous uses for the dog. Certain breeds are more suited to police work than others, with herding and gun-dog breeds being particularly popular choices. Intelligence, obedience, agility and natural instincts are the most important canine characteristics sought by the police.

▲ Disciplined but formidable, many breeds, such as German Sherperds, are invaluable in police crowd control.

Crowd Control and Public Order

The most common usage of dogs in police forces is in controlling the movement of large groups of people. Sporting events, protests and public meetings often require a police presence and, to reinforce that presence, the police will commonly employ dogs. German Shepherds, Belgian Shepherds and sometimes other breeds will be at the side of their handler – equipped and trained to restrain and hold any person that breaches the peace or poses a threat to public safety. The dogs have to be self-controlled and obedient but capable of neutralizing any threats posed by people or crowds. Often, the bark of a well-trained police dog is enough to deter a would-be criminal.

Contraband Detection

Drugs, illegal firearms and counterfeit goods are unlikely to get past the well-trained and highly sensitive nose of a police contraband-detection dog. Springer Spaniels,

Labradors and Cocker Spaniels are commonly used by border-control and airport officers in order to stem the flow of such contraband. The dogs are trained from an early age to respond to the scent of an illegal item. The dogs will typically sit, or otherwise indicate to their handler that they have a scent. Some dogs have been trained to detect the ink used in counterfeit currency.

Explosives Detection

In order to ensure public safety there is an elite group of specially trained explosives detection dogs patrolling the world's streets and corridors. Explosive detection dogs have to be specially trained to 'freeze' when they identify an explosive. An over-excited or curious dog could end up activating any explosive devices if it does not immediately hold its movement. This abrupt coming to a halt is a sure sign to the handler that the dog has a find. Dogs that are trained to find explosives are able to identify the scent through a brick wall.

Personal Security

Due to the nature of police work some officers require personal dogs for their own security. German Shepherds and Belgian Shepherds are

◄ Dogs are trained by the armed forces to detect explosives and to freeze immediately on discovering a device.

ideal for this due to their agility, loyalty and obedience. Many dogs have given up their own lives to protect their handlers.

Cadaver Detection

One of the more unpleasant aspects of police dog work is that of the cadaver- or human-remains detection dog. Many cases of murder and abduction have been brought to their grizzly conclusions by well-trained dogs. Popular breeds for this work include scent hounds, such as the Basset Hound and Bloodhound, as well as gun-dog breeds such as the Springer and Cocker Spaniels. Although this work does not prevent crime, it does help bring prosecutions against criminals and enables families to know exactly what happened to a victim. The dogs are specially trained and highly skilled, enabling them to detect the chemicals that a body gives off during decomposition.

Escapee or Missing Person Detection

Bloodhounds and other scent-hound breeds are often used to find escaped criminals. Bloodhounds have exceptionally powerful noses and will find someone hiding miles away, over many different types of terrain. The dogs are trained not to harm any escapees they find, but to hold them. If the dog is tracking a missing person, they will be commanded to either signal the find or to assist the missing person if they are in need of help.

◄ Bloodhounds scenting a trail; once they find a missing person, the Bloodhound will remain with him or her until human assistance arrives.

Herding Dogs

Humans and dogs have a strong history of cooperation. We have put dogs to work in many roles, developing and refining their instincts and abilities to enable us to evolve together. One of the most important jobs dogs have performed for us is herding. Before refrigeration food had to be moved around for trading before it was killed; with livestock transportation came the need to protect and guard the valuable herds – help that dogs could preovide.

Herding Breeds

As our habits and needs changed, so did the jobs of the livestock-herding dogs. Some were bred to protect, some were bred to herd in fields and others were bred to help with travel. The commonest type of

job performed by herding or pastoral breeds was that of the sheepdog. Sheepdogs have two main functions, to herd and to drove. Herding is done in a field under a shepherd's instruction, while droving is done in order to move flocks through towns and villages. Other functions of herding or pastoral breeds include flock watch dogs (bred for their alertness) and flock guard dogs (bred for strength and tenacity). Popular pet breeds that were originally bred for herding include the Anatolian Shepherd Dog, the Australian Cattle Dog, the Australian Shepherd, the Belgian Shepherd and the Border Collie.

◄ Droving dogs were bred to help shepherds and cowherds move their livestock safely along the lanes from field to market.

► Adult Briards are intelligent and swift, making them ideal herders to help a shepherd pen his flock.

▲ Both guarding and herding instincts were bred in the Anatolian Shepherd Dog, so they could protect their flocks from wolves and bears.

Herders

Many of the most intelligent and agile breeds today derive from herding stock. The German Shepherd, Border Collie and Briard were all bred to assist a shepherd with his flock. The dogs were required to put the sheep back into their pens and move them around the fields and farms at the shepherd's command.

Drovers

In order for shepherds and farmers to trade their livestock, they needed to be able to move it as a group from place to place. This required the skill and determination of a specially bred droving dog, such as an Old English Sheepdog or Border Collie. The shepherd would have a set of commands that he would use to control the movement of the flock or herd through the actions of his dog. The dogs would instinctively be driven to nip at the heels of any livestock that was breaking away from the herd.

Protectors

The type of environment in which a dog worked determined the role it would need to play. Herding dogs based in places where predators were large, such as wolves and big cats, would need to be even bigger and more fearless than that predator in order to keep the herd safe. The Anatolian Shepherd Dog was bred specifically to protect herds from wolves and bears. Guarding and herding instincts were bred into these dogs to ensure that they could fulfil both roles.

Modern Herding Breeds

Today the need for herding dogs is relatively small compared to the actual number of herding dogs in existence. Herding breeds make popular pets due to their intelligence and temperament. Border Collies, German Shepherds and various breeds of sheepdog are now just as popular as companion animals as they once were for their working abilities.

Competition

Despite fulfilling the role of pet, most herding or pastoral breeds retain strong herding instincts. This is why herding competition is so popular today. Sheepdog trials and agility contests are designed to judge and assess the abilities of the trainer as well as the latent instincts of the herding dogs.

Exploiting the Herding Instinct

Despite being bred originally for pastoral or herding purposes, many of the skills and attributes of herding dogs have been applied to more modern requirements. German Shepherds make fantastic guard and assistance dogs due to their instincts for protecting a pack. Their agility enables them to perform this function better than many breeds.

◀ Intelligent and fiercely loyal, German Shepherd dogs make ideal assistance dogs in a wide variety of situations.

Gun Dogs and Hound Packs

Sometimes we forget that our pet dogs were once highly skilled working animals. Many of the most popular pet breeds in the world were once favoured for their abilities to hunt and help us gather food. The dogs have not lost any of those instincts, but often they do not need to use them any more. When we domesticated our dogs and started to keep them as pets, we relieved them of their duties and encouraged them to settle into retirement. However, with Springer Spaniels able to detect cancer in humans and Bloodhounds able to find people trapped in collapsed buildings, who knows what the future holds.

▲ Many of the most intelligent, good-natured breeds are now simply owned as much-loved pets and companions.

Traditional Gun Dogs

Breeds associated with shooting, otherwise referred to as gun dogs, have extremely strong instincts to retrieve, which is why they love to fetch a stick or ball. Some of the most popular and well-known gun-dog breeds are Labrador Retrievers, Golden Retrievers, Springer Spaniels, Cocker Spaniels, Pointers and Weimaraners.

There were many different jobs for a gun dog, from flushing the birds up into the air to retrieving game that had been shot. Each gun dog breed was a specialist at a certain job, which is why some of the breeds have very specific names, such as the Nova Scotia Duck Tolling Retriever.

The skills that were developed and trained when dogs were required to work are now being put to use in the modern world. Intelligence, obedience and an ability to

follow instructions make gun dogs the ideal choice for assistance work. This is why many of the guide dogs that work today are Labrador Retrievers.

Modern Gun Dogs

Shooting is still a popular activity and dogs play a large part in making it enjoyable for the participants. Many people make a good living out of training and supplying the best gun dogs to shooting parties. Though not as popular or necessary today as it was in the past, shooting and hunting still provides work for many talented and intelligent dogs.

Hound Packs

Hounds come in three types – those that use their sight, those that use their sense of smell and those that combine both. Sight hounds are fast, lean and athletic, which would have enabled them to chase down quarry across long distances to win food for their masters. Greyhounds and Salukis are good examples of this.

Scent hounds are bigger and stronger but traditionally relied on their tracking abilities to find prey, even if it was hiding. Today, there is still call for the skills of a scent hound. Man has not managed to invent anything to rival

◄ Pointers were bred as gun dogs to point to the game and then, just as retrievers do, to retrieve it while on a shoot.

► Salukis are both lean and swift. They were originally bred to hunt gazelle in the deserts of Arabia.

the awesome power of the canine nose. Sight hounds are less in demand, but still bring pleasure and satisfaction to many through competing in races.

Hunting parties often use packs of hounds. Fox hunts traditionally incorporate packs of scent hounds, normally Beagles and Basset Hounds, that use a combination of sight and scent to find and flush out foxes. This is a controversial pursuit and is not as popular as it once was, having been banned to various degrees in certain countries.

Modern Hounds

Members of the hound group were once used to chase and catch prey, which is why they love to run when we let them off the lead. Hounds make fantastic pets due to their innate loyalty and obedience. They will retain strong instincts but in the hands of a confident trainer they adapt brilliantly to domestic life.

► In packs of hounds, the Beagles, and sometimes Basset Hounds, work together, led by an Alpha – the dominant male in the pack.

Performing Dogs

People are often amazed at the agility and level of training that some dogs can achieve. Heelwork, obedience and Schutzhund (a sport that tests a dog's training and behaviour) are just some of the ways in which dogs perform for our enjoyment. Since dogs often are not required to work any more it is through demonstrating, competing and performing for our pleasure that they can display their instinctive talents. Many hours of training goes into preparing dogs for performance – it is a serious business.

Heel Work

Heel work is an activity that measures a dog's ability to perform certain routines on command. Herding breeds such as Border Collies and German Shepherds are good at this due to their keen intelligence and ability to learn. Trainers teach dogs specific commands for each move and put together an impressive sequence, which is then judged by a panel of experts.

Obedience

Competitive obedience sees highly trained and intelligent dogs responding to complex and demanding instructions. Basic obedience, such as teaching a dog to

▶ Heelwork requires a dog to be trained to perform impressive sequences of actions, often, as here, performed to music.

stay, is commonplace, but in competitive obedience dogs are required to perform tasks involving all manner of skills. Finding hidden items, solving problems and resisting instinct are all measures of a dog's obedience.

Instinct-based Performance

Every dog has a set of core working instincts. Displaying those instincts in a competition is an ideal way for us to enjoy the abilities and talents of our dogs. Gun dogs compete in field trials, herding breeds compete in sheepdog trials and Greyhounds compete in races. One of the most important aspects of this type of performance is the integrity with which a dog represents its skill. Certain breeds are equipped to perform varied roles, but in the context of instinct-based performance it is essential that the dogs perform in a traditional manner.

Schutzhund

Schutzhund was developed in Germany to test the abilities of German Shepherd Dogs. Up until then dogs were judged on appearance only. It combines elements of agility, obedience and protection and is commonly used by police forces to test the abilities of prospective dogs. German Shepherds, Belgian Shepherds and Border Collies frequently perform in Schutzhund competitions – a very popular spectator sport.

Circus Dogs

Dog acts were traditionally a popular part of circus performances. Today it is rare to see dogs in circus performances, but they have certainly made their mark on performing history. Poodles were popular as canine clown performers due to their combination of striking looks and agility. Jumping through hoops, balancing acts and performing in magic tricks are all jobs that circus dogs have undertaken.

▶ Problem solving and finding hidden items are just some of the skills required of a dog in competitive obedience trials.

Dogs on the Stage

Many popular theatre productions have included dogs. Specially trained dogs, often members of performers' unions, have been used in stage productions of *The Wizard of Oz*, *Little Orphan Annie* and even Shakespeare plays.

Private Entertainers

Throughout history people have sought the company of dogs for entertainment. In medieval Europe rich and important figures who had far to travel would often take a servant and a dog in order for a performance to be delivered to relieve the boredom of the journey. Noblemen and leaders have often called upon the services of dogs to provide them with fun and amusement. Centuries ago rich Italians would dress up their pet Pugs in pantaloons to provide them with amusement.

Novelty Performances

Many pet dogs achieve fame with their unusual and quirky abilities. One notable example is Tyson the skateboarding Bulldog. Tyson's owner published footage on the Internet of him skating, which led to cult fame for the talented dog. He went on to appear on *The Oprah Winfrey Show*, where he performed in front of a massive American TV audience.

▶ A popular breed in dog circuses, Poodles are nimble and biddable and are able to learn skills such as skipping.

Dogs and Royalty

From King Canute to the current Queen of England, dogs and royalty have always been inseparable. New breeds have been brought into existence on the whim of past kings, and other breeds reserved for ownership by royal decree only. Were it not for the Shang Dynasty and one emperor's desires we would not have the Pug, while the Cavalier King Charles Spaniel owes its existence to the royal who created the breed.

King Canute (1016–35)

King Canute, the second Dane to rule England, invented the concept of toy dogs. He passed a law making it illegal for large dogs to be used in hunting, in order to make it fairer on the prey. Because of this, breeders went to great efforts to use only the smallest mating stock, until the breed known at the time as the Toy Spaniel was established. This breed went on to be a forefather of the Cavalier King Charles Spaniel.

King James I (1603–25)

King James I, who was ruling monarch of England, Scotland and Ireland, loved dogs. He had many hunting hounds, but his particular favourite was a dog named Jewel. Sadly she was found dead, killed by a single bullet. The King was outraged to find out that the killer was his wife, Queen Anne, who had accidentally shot Jewel while deer hunting.

◄ The Cavalier King Charles Spaniel is the descendant of the Toy Spaniel created by King Canute.

► Avid dog-lover, King James I, hunting with his daughter in Greenwich Park. Ackerman print (1838) by unnamed artist.

King Charles II (1660–85)

King Charles II was known as Cavalier King Charles due to the way in which he dealt with his parliament. He was also known for his love of dogs. One dog in particular, a Toy Spaniel, was often prescribed to the sick by doctors (its warming presence on the lap was deemed to help fight a cold). The breed was later renamed the Cavalier King Charles Spaniel in honour of its most powerful admirer

Prince William of Orange (1689–94)

This Dutch aristocrat, who later became King William III, was a big admirer of Pugs. He travelled with them from England to Holland, where he resided at the House of Orange. When the Dutch repelled a Spanish invasion shortly before the Prince became King of England he believed the good fortune was down to the dog, which became the official symbol of the House of Orange.

Queen Victoria (1837–1901)

Queen Victoria played a large part in developing a popular modern breed. In the 1700s, Queen Charlotte, wife of George III, had already brought to England a white dog, from the area of eastern Germany once known as Pomerania. Victoria later owned similar dogs – perhaps descended from Charlotte's – and, upon the death of her husband Prince Albert in 1861, she focused

◄ King Charles II as a boy, pictured with an adored pet dog. Painting by Sir Anthony van Dyck.

► Queen Victoria's pet Pomeranian, named Turi, seen here in 1899, was at her bedside when she died in 1901.

her attention on tending to them. Concerned with their size, she bred them with smaller breeds to establish the dog known today as the Pomeranian.

King George V (1910–36)

King George V founded the House of Windsor and was Grandfather of the current Queen of England. He loved Sealyham Terriers and Cairn Terriers and many royally commissioned paintings picture him doting on his dogs.

Queen Elizabeth II (1952–present)

The reigning British monarch is possibly the most well-known royal dog lover. Currently the Queen has ten dogs: Emma, Linnet, Holly and Willow are the names of her Corgis; she also has three 'Dorgis' – a cross between a Dachshund and a Corgi.

Queen Elizabeth has owned more than 30 Corgis. The first was Susan, given to her on her 18th birthday by her father, King George VI. The Queen is a keen dog trainer and is well known for her admiration of working gun-dog breeds, such as Springer Spaniels.

◄ George, Duke of York, (the future King George V) c. 1895 encouraging his pet to beg for a tidbit.

► Queen Elizabeth II has owned many dogs over the years, favouring the Corgi, as seen here at Sandringham, Norfolk, 1970.

Evolution and Domestication

It is a misconception that man domesticated the dog. Man in fact domesticated the wolf, and the offspring of the domesticated wolf evolved into the dogs of today. Under man's guidance dogs have been bred, inter-bred and cross-bred to create new bloodlines and to improve on old ones. Breeds have come and gone, disappearing into extinction as their value diminished; other breeds have remained wild, unable to find a role alongside man. Even today new breeds are becoming established to fulfil our need for companionship.

The Start of Selective Breeding

More than 15,000 years ago different tribes came into contact with wolves as they migrated over landmasses. One of the first things man noticed about the wolf was its ability as a hunter. As man evolved he realized that

◄ Nature played its part in the evolution of the dog, equipping Huskys, for instance, with incredibly thick coats for freezing conditions.

► The Timber Wolf. Gradually, through many generations of selective breeding, an ideal hunting partner was bred: the dog.

alongside the wolf he could improve his own chances of survival and evolution. However, it was not to happen quickly – it took generations of wolves and men coming into contact before the latter could impose any influence. As man noticed characteristics in the wolf that were of value to him, he attempted to make these more prominent through a process known as selective breeding.

Two strong wolves bred together would create even stronger offspring, while an intelligent wolf and a fast wolf would, in theory, create fast and intelligent descendants. Things did not always go to plan and sometimes the intended offspring would turn out weak, sickly and of no use to humans. In other cases results would occur that man did not plan, but that benefited him nonetheless.

The First Dogs

As the wolf species diversified, the generations of new wolves began to look more and more different from the wolves with which man had first come into contact. As these new animals evolved, man's ability to select desirable mating partnerships improved. Nature played its part too, equipping wolves living in cold climates with thick coats. It was a long process, but man was able to control it to a certain extent. Eventually the animals were sufficiently different to the original wolves to serve man's changing needs; these animals were the original domesticated dogs.

◄ Having a strong desire to help defend the pack, dogs make ideal look-out sentries and guards.

► There are approximately nine breeds of wolf, of which the Grey Wolf (shown) is one.

The Evolution of the Canine

As the needs of the human race changed, man was able to produce and train dogs capable of helping and serving. Man was able to control livestock with a dog, so only dogs that displayed the ability to do this were used for breeding. If the offspring did not match the desires of man they would be abandoned. Gradually humans became able to produce dogs that catered for very specific needs. Swimming ability was valued as man realized the importance of water in early farming and travel. When man began to establish modern dwellings he required dogs of courage and strength to protect them.

The Modern Canine

Every breed of dog was bred for a purpose and these purposes or jobs are used to define the breed groups we know today. Herding, hunting, protecting, retrieving and transporting were all skills for which man needed

a dog. Although we may no longer require all these services, the dog still proves to be of value by combining skills from the past and applying them to modern needs. The most valuable asset a dog offers today's society is companionship. Some dogs were bred specifically for companionship, while others have adapted to provide company as their original duties ceased to exist. It is amazing to consider that from the wolf came both the tiny Yorkshire Terrier and the giant St Bernard.

◄ It is amazing that the tiny Yorkshire Terrier's ancestral line reaches back to the wolf.

► While large, like the wolf, the St Bernard is renowned for its biddable nature and ability to undertake complicated mountain-rescue operations

Pedigree and Non-Pedigree Dogs

A pedigree is a document that confirms the ancestry and heritage of a pure-bred dog. Any dog that has a pedigree is classified as a pedigree dog or pure-bred. Having a pedigree enables a person to see the lineage and parentage of a dog and the value of a dog is affected by the strength of that pedigree. If the dog descends from notable specimens, such as champions or conformation winners, its value may increase. Pedigrees, typically, are administered by the national kennel club of the country in which the dog was born.

Pedigree and Pure-bred

Any dog that conforms to a set type of a breed tends to be named by that breed. In the true sense, for a dog to be a pure-bred or pedigree it must have a lineage of only members of its breed. It is down to the governing body in the relevant country to issue pedigrees and the criteria used vary from organization to organization. Naturally, if a

▶ The Lhasa Apso is generally a very healthy breed, but the most common complaint is kidney disease.

dog is descended only from members of its own type there is a significantly higher incidence of in-breeding. Inbreeding is caused when closely related dogs mate and the offspring may exhibit signs of weak genetics. The more inbreeding that occurs, the more likely a breed is to develop health problems.

Pedigree dogs conform to a physical and characteristic type. They will be roughly the same size throughout the breed and will have the same set of working instincts. This is one of the reasons people favour pedigree dogs over non-pedigree dogs.

Non-Pedigree Dogs

Dogs that are not issued with a pedigree certificate are non-pedigree dogs. Non-pedigree dogs include crossbreeds, mixed breeds or mongrels and mutts. Typically non-pedigree dogs have a more diverse gene pool, which commonly means they are of more robust health and live longer. Although there is little or

no uniformity among non-pedigree dogs in terms of appearance, many people favour their more rugged look.

Crossbreeds

A crossbreed is the name given to the offspring of two purebred dogs of different breeds. For example, if a Labrador Retriever and German Shepherd Dog mate, the

◄ An adorable scruffy mutt. Crossbreeds can live healthier lives than pedigrees, avoiding the weaknesses inherent in inbreeding.

► A crossbreed showing the long fur on the muzzle typical of the Bearded Collie and the darker colouring of the Border Collie.

offspring will not be purely one breed, even if they inherit their appearance from only one parent. Normally the offspring will inherit physical and mental attributes from both parents. Many true breeds came about from crossbreeding, only to be established as a breed in its own right when the offspring displayed uniformity with sufficient regularity. It is often desired for two different breeds to mate for working purposes, so that the offspring inherit appealing qualities of both parents. Some crosses are deliberately carried out to create so-called 'designer' dog breeds. Popular crosses of this nature include the Labra-doodle (Labrador and Poodle) and Puggle (Pug and Beagle).

Mixed Breeds

Mixed breeds are dogs that are of unknown or undeterminable heritage. A mixed-breed dog will have visible signs of heritage from more than two breeds. This can mean that the dog's parents were crossbreeds or mixed breeds. In some cases it is possible to identify certain aspects of a dog's heritage through factors such as colour, size, coat or head shape. Mixed-breed dogs are less uniform than crossbreeds and pedigree dogs, but are generally healthier.

Mixed-breed dogs are also known as 'mongrels', 'mutts' or 'curs'. Most dogs that are of such mixed parentage are more or less individual. Some inherit more characteristics from one parent than the other, while other mixed breeds inherit equal amounts of physical characteristics from both parents. In some instances mixed breeds go on to become established breeds in their own right. For example, in some countries the Jack Russell Terrier used to be known as the Parson Russell Terrier, or a cross of that breed.

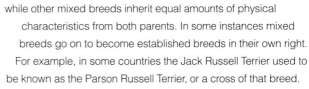

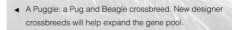

◀ A Puggle: a Pug and Beagle crossbreed. New designer crossbreeds will help expand the gene pool.

Breed Development

It is amazing to look at the huge Great Dane and the tiny Chihuahua and consider that they evolved from the same animal. There are few animal species on Earth that display such a degree of physical diversity as the domestic dog. This is mainly due to man having controlled dog breeding since ancient times. The development of individual breeds is a long process that goes through many stages. There are environmental, social, natural and even political factors that influence the development of dog breeds.

Necessity

The first stage of the development of a dog breed is when man identifies a need or desire for a certain type of dog. Whether it is a herding dog that can work in the cold or a companion dog that is small and alert, every dog breed has come into existence because man identified a need for it. It may be that a dog existed that only partly fulfilled a need and was then used to develop a new, more suitable breed. Some entirely new breed groups have come into existence due to man's need for a certain type of dog.

◄ Each breed of dog has been bred to meet a need in man; whether to help herd sheep, or simply for companionship.

Selective Breeding

The next step is when man breeds certain dogs with other dogs to generate a set of desired characteristics. This happened when man domesticated the wolf and it happened when Louis Dobermann wanted an agile, strong and fearless guard dog for protection. It takes generations for the desired characteristics to present themselves consistently, but when they do the dogs with the strongest likeness to man's original plan are used for breeding. The dogs are tried and tested in the role that they were bred for, with the most suitable being used to continue the bloodline.

Breeding True

'Breeding true' is a term that is applied to the stage of development where the majority of dogs are of a predictable and controlled appearance and temperament. This is where the breed begins to exhibit uniform characteristics, such as coat colour, size, temperament and intelligence level, that will become typical of that breed.

Standardization

A breed becomes standardized when an agreed set of criteria is written that governs how the dog shall look and act. It is often done in the form of an official breed standard administered by one of the many national kennel clubs. A dog can be in existence for centuries before it reaches the stage of standardization.

Acceptance

When a breed becomes accepted by an official governing body, such as the UK Kennel Club or the Fédération Cynologique Internationale, it becomes an officially recognized breed. Even today there are old and established breeds that are yet to be recognized by foreign organizations or even their own

kennel club or equivalent body. This can be due to social or political reasons or simply because the dog is not present in high enough numbers in that particular part of the world.

Popularity

Each dog breed will attain a different level of mainstream popularity. The Labrador Retriever and the German Shepherd Dog, for example, have achieved worldwide popularity as both pets and working dogs. They exist in almost all parts of the world and are instantly recognizable as being of their type. Other breeds are less well known, offering a more specific or niche appeal to owners. The popularity of breeds declines and increases under the influence of our own lifestyles. Fighting breeds are less popular because dog fighting itself is now socially unacceptable.

Herding breeds tend to be constantly popular due to their versatility and intelligence, which enables them to function in many different and varied roles.

◄ Labrador Retrievers are globally popular, with appeal and characteristics that make them suitable as both domestic pets and working dogs.

► These Irish Soft Coated Wheaten Terrier pups are identical, showing that that pedigree line is 'breeding true'.

Early Dog Care

The dog is a valuable asset to man and has been for centuries. As such, the animal has been subject to special care and devotion. Concepts such as boarding, veterinary care and obedience training are comparatively new, while the practices of grooming, selective breeding and husbandry have their foundations further back in history. Necessity for more effective workers or stronger and healthier breeding stock was the main motivation for early dog care.

Veterinary Care

Fossilized remains suggest that early man was capable of treating injured or sick dogs. The concept of husbandry preceded the practice of veterinary medicine, which did not arise in Europe until as recently as the eighteenth century. Resting dogs with disease and treating injuries with splints and compression are early examples of husbandry. Good animal husbandry is still a very important element of modern dog care.

◀ Illustration of the Care and Diseases of Hunting Dogs, after Gaston Phoebus, 1387–89. In the Middles Ages, dog care was vital when the dogs were of practical use.

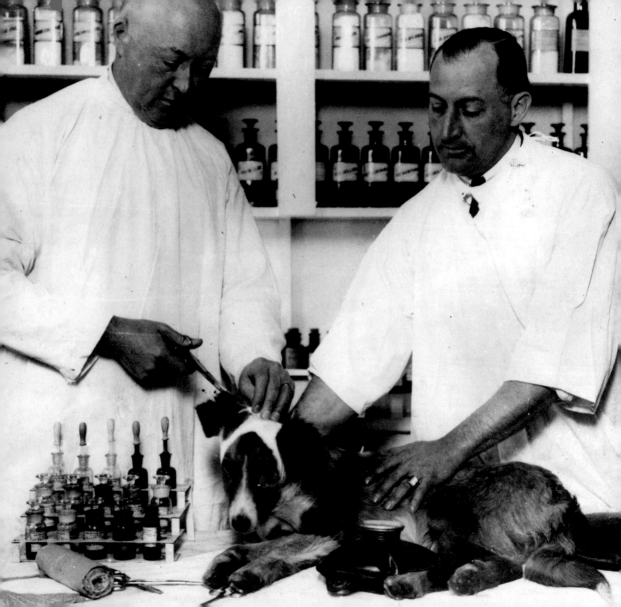

Grooming

Early grooming was not done for cosmetic reasons but for practical working reasons. A case in point is the Poodle. Modern Poodles are groomed to reflect contemporary tastes and styles, but many of these styles originate from genuine working necessities. The early working Poodle was a water-going dog, bred for a dense and curly coat to provide warmth. However, having a dense coat meant that the dog struggled in water so the coat was often clipped with only the joints such as the knees and elbows left coated. This gave rise to a distinctive pom-pom appearance on these parts of the body, which is still popular as a style today.

Specialized Feeding

Throughout the ages of primitive dog ownership dogs ate what they killed. It was rare for early man ever to part with food and even rarer for him to willingly give food to his dog. As time went by and dogs were valued as more than just hunters, it was necessary for

◄ Grooming is always important: the traditional pom-pom Poodle clip was developed to protect the joints of these water dogs.

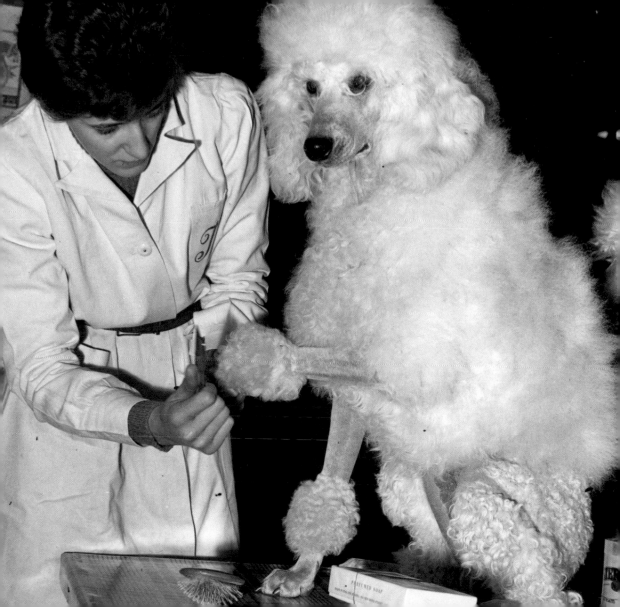

their owners to provide food so that the dog could work. Much of the time this was limited to leftover scraps and carcasses.

Dogs in the wild are omnivorous, but mainly eat meat. They get their vegetable intake from gorging on the decaying food in the stomachs of their prey. When this was recognized by humans, vegetation and cereal-based food was often included in the canine diet. Dogs are robust and can eat most things, so feeding has only become specialized very recently when technology and lifestyle permitted it.

Selective Breeding

Selective breeding is the cornerstone of the canine's evolution – without it the domesticated dog of modern times would not exist. The concept of selective breeding began in a very primitive fashion, with large specimens being matched with strong specimens. But as the needs of mankind evolved we sought new and more complex ways of breeding dogs. Crossing terrier-type dogs with larger, heavier breeds gave rise to formidable hunting and guarding dogs. Only recently has the concept of breeding for appearance become relevant. In the past, any selective breeding was done to produce the healthiest, strongest, most intelligent and capable dogs possible.

Training

Dogs are instinctive and man has had very little need to instruct the dog. Upon noticing strong instincts that would prove to be of value, man encouraged that dog to reproduce. Guiding a dog to perform a certain role is a very new phenomenon and historically dogs that were of no working use were abandoned. Punishment for failure and reward for success – the two commonest ways of training today – were used in early dog training. However, concepts such as conditioning (learning consequences through repetition) and advanced reinforcement (rewarding or discouraging actions by providing or removing a stimulus) were not considered useful until the dog became domesticated.

How Dogs work

Anatomy, Physiology and Appearance

By studying the physical make-up of a dog it is possible to observe the way in which nature equipped this animal to survive and evolve. Eyes designed for spotting danger at a distance, a keen sense of smell in order to seek out prey and teeth shaped for tearing open a carcass are just three of the reasons that the canine has been an evolutionary success. Man has influenced the appearance of the dog through selective breeding, but it took nature thousands of years to create the animal that man has found so valuable.

Skeleton and Physique

The dog comes in many shapes and sizes but its skeletal anatomy typically is uniform from breed to breed. All dogs have around 319 bones, with length being the only distinguishing factor between breeds – particularly in the leg bones. The front and hind legs' form and function are different from each other, with the hind legs being stronger but less flexible. Discernible differences in anatomy between breeds are due normally to the size of certain bones and the muscle mass in certain parts of the body.

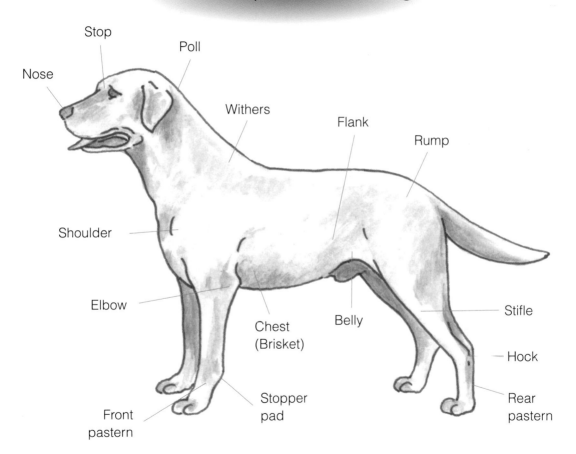

External points of the dog

Stop

Poll

Nose

Withers

Flank

Rump

Shoulder

Elbow

Chest
(Brisket)

Belly

Stifle

Hock

Front
pastern

Stopper
pad

Rear
pastern

The Skeleton

Skull The shape and size of the canine skull varies from breed to breed, but it is typically long to the muzzle and dome-shaped at the top.

Cervical vertebrae These are the bones in a dog's neck; some breeds display longer necks than others.

Thoracic vertebrae These are the spinal bones that run from the bottom of the neck to the middle of the back, covering the same area as the chest.

Lumbar vertebrae These are the spinal bones that run from the middle of the back to the base of the tail.

Sacrum This is the set of bones located in the rump.

Caudal vertebrae These are the bones that form the tail; they do not run to the tip of the tail.

Pelvis This enables mobility; it is located above the hind legs.

Femur This is the bone that forms the top part of the hind leg, going up from the knee to the pelvis.

Fibula This is one of the two bones that form the lower part of the hind leg.

Tibia This is the other bone that forms the lower part of the hind leg.

Tarsus This is the heel bone that leads from the paw to the lower part of the hind leg.

Metatarsus The metatarsal bones form the basis of the rear paw.

Phalange This is the bone that occurs in the canine digits, of which there are three on each paw.

Metacarpus The metacarpal bones form the front paw; its movement is more flexible than that of the hind paw.

Carpus This is the wrist bone of the front leg; the carpus enables greater flexibility of the metacarpus.

Ulna This is one of the two bones of the lower part of the front leg.

Radius This is the other bone in the lower front leg.

Humerus This large bone forms the uppermost part of the front leg.

Rib This is part of the rib cage; the dog has 13 ribs.

Scapula This is the shoulder bone, located at the top of the front legs.

Lower maxillary This bone forms the lower part of the jaw, independent of the skull.

Orbit This is the eye cavity; these cavities are shaped differently from breed to breed.

Skeleton of the dog

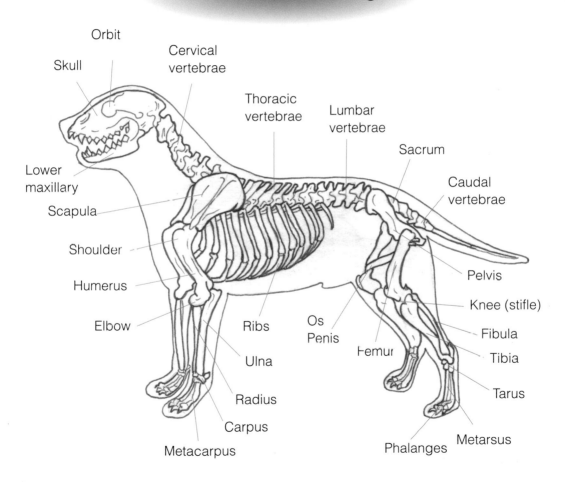

Orbit

Skull

Cervical vertebrae

Thoracic vertebrae

Lumbar vertebrae

Sacrum

Caudal vertebrae

Lower maxillary

Scapula

Shoulder

Humerus

Elbow

Ribs

Os Penis

Femur

Pelvis

Knee (stifle)

Fibula

Tibia

Tarus

Ulna

Radius

Carpus

Metacarpus

Phalanges

Metarsus

Physique

Physical differences between dogs are created by differences in length and in the mass of muscles. All dogs possess the same skeletal form – the differences in physique, shape and build relate to the formation and size of certain muscle groups compared to others.

Herding breeds are typically lean, with well-proportioned but not bulky thigh muscles. Molosser breeds such as the Rottweiler tend to have dense muscles throughout the body, but particularly in the chest and hind legs.

Sight hound breeds typically have leaner muscles that are longer in order to increase propulsion when running. Dogs that are bred for strength tend to have shorter leg bones in relation to the rest of the body in order to lower their centre of gravity.

Internal Make-Up

The internal make-up of a dog is typical of most omnivorous land mammals of its size. Through evolution the dog has developed a group of internal systems that

◄ Molosser breeds, such as Rottweilers, are heavily built, thick chested and with sturdy haunches.

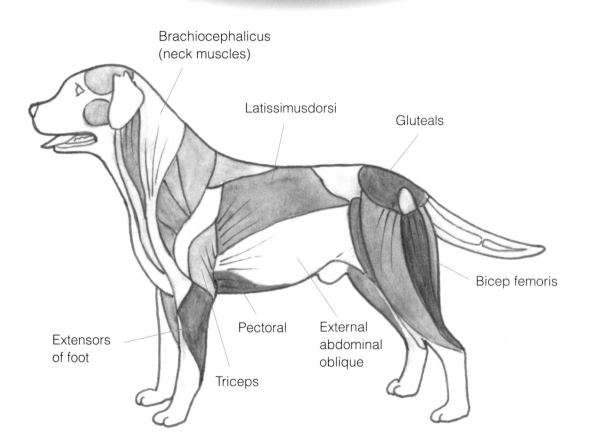

Muscular system of the dog

Brachiocephalicus
(neck muscles)

Latissimusdorsi

Gluteals

Bicep femoris

Extensors
of foot

Pectoral

Triceps

External
abdominal
oblique

perform functions essential to growth and survival. Deficiencies in these systems lead to illness and, in extreme cases, death if veterinary care is not delivered. Some conditions relating to the cardiovascular and digestive systems are the result of modern breeding methods, others are more widespread through the animal kingdom and are not a result of human actions.

Cardiovascular System

The cardiovascular system includes the heart and blood vessels. It is responsible for pumping blood through the body, enabling the rest of the body's organs and extremities to function. The heart is located in between the tops of the front legs. The typical resting heart rate for a healthy dog is 70–120 beats per minute. Inherited heart problems are common in certain breeds – notably the Bulldog, which has a lower life expectancy today than it used to.

Digestive System

The digestive system performs the functions of ingesting, digesting and eliminating food products from the body. Externally the digestive system comprises the mouth, teeth and tongue. Internally the digestive system is made up of, from mouth to tail, the oesophagus, stomach, small intestine, large intestine, pancreas, colon, liver and gall bladder. The canine digestive system is robust and can handle food that would make

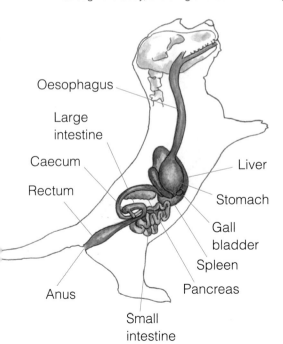

Oesophagus

Large
intestine

Caecum

Rectum

Liver

Stomach

Gall
bladder

Spleen

Pancreas

Anus

Small
intestine

◀ Digestive system of the dog

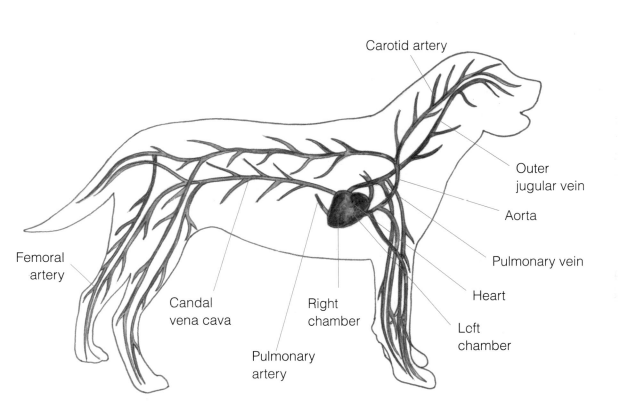

Cardiovascular system of the dog

Carotid artery

Outer
jugular vein

Aorta

Pulmonary vein

Heart

Left
chamber

Right
chamber

Candal
vena cava

Pulmonary
artery

Femoral
artery

humans very sick. The stomach of a canine is long and relatively narrow, which means that it is prone to gastric torsion – a condition that can lead to severe illness and death if not treated. This is more common in large-breed dogs, such as the Rottweiler.

Integumentary System

This is the organ system that governs the skin and fur. It is a very important part of the canine body as it controls insulation; it is also the largest organ in the body. Dogs do not sweat through the skin, only through the paw pads and nose. They also lose water through the tongue when panting.

Respiratory System

The respiratory system governs the intake of oxygen and breathing. It is also the system responsible for expelling waste gas and regulating body temperature. The normal body temperature for a healthy dog is 100.5–102.5 Fahrenheit (38–39.2 Celsius). The internal elements of the respiratory system are the trachea and lungs, and externally the mouth and nose.

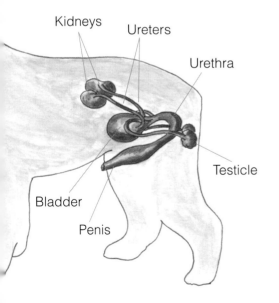

Kidneys Ureters Urethra Testicle Bladder Penis

Urogenital System

This system includes the sex organs and the urinary excretion organs – the kidneys, bladder, urethra and

◀ Urogenital system of the male dog

Respiratory system of the dog

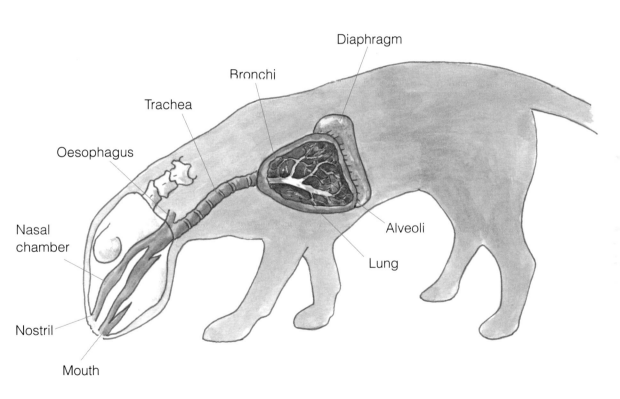

Diaphragm

Bronchi

Trachea

Oesophagus

Nasal
chamber

Nostril

Mouth

Alveoli

Lung

▲ The Bloodhound has more nerve endings in its nose than other breeds, enhancing sense of smell.

genitalia. Its function is two-fold: to facilitate reproduction and to remove waste from the blood.

Nervous System

The nervous system controls the rest of the body. It governs movement, instinct, impulse and reflex. It enables the nerves inside the body to function and the organs to operate and is made up of the brain, spinal chord and nerves. The canine's nervous system has evolved to enable it to react quickly to impulses and instincts.

Endocrine System

The endocrine system governs the function of the organs through the distribution of hormones. It is made up of thyroid glands, adrenal glands and parathyroid glands.

Differences between Breeds

There are few fundamental differences between the inner workings of different dog breeds but breeding and evolution has influenced certain parts of the body to function to a higher level than others in different breeds. For example some breeds, such as the Bloodhound, have more nerve endings in their noses, which enables them to have a more sensitive sense of smell. Other breeds, such as German Shepherds, may have higher tolerance to cold or pain, which enables them to function better in their working role.

Nervous system of the dog

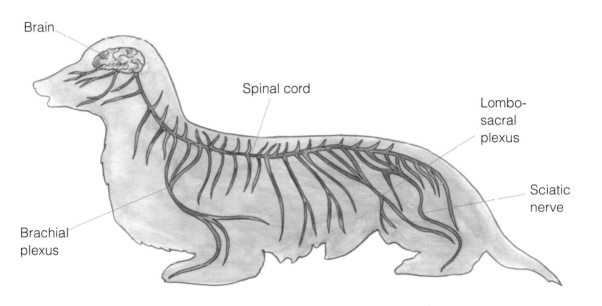

Brain

Spinal cord

Lombo-
sacral
plexus

Sciatic
nerve

Brachial
plexus

Skull, Teeth and Nails

The canine skull is one of the most distinguishing factors between breeds. The shape of the skull has influence on the senses of sight, hearing and smell. It also influences a breed's ability to deliver a bite and has ramifications in terms of how well a breed can defend itself against attack. The teeth are essential for feeding and defending – poor teeth would lead to death in the wild. Good oral health in dogs is essential to prevent wider health problems throughout the body.

The Skull

Evolution primarily influenced skull shape, with inherited skull shapes and sizes coming from the original wolves that were used to breed the first domesticated dogs. Human intervention, such as breeding dogs with pronounced skull shapes to produce dogs with larger skulls, has led to a wide diversification in shape.

Different Skull Shapes

There are two main shapes of the canine skull: one is long and narrow with a long muzzle, the other is rounder, with a heavier jaw and a more pronounced dome at the top. However, there are many different variants in between these two extremes. Face shape is also widely diverse between breeds – this is affected to an extent by skull shape but is also influenced by weight, fur type and breeding.

▶ The skull shape, size and proportion are key to defining a breed and to determining how a dog can feed and defend itself.

Selection of skull types

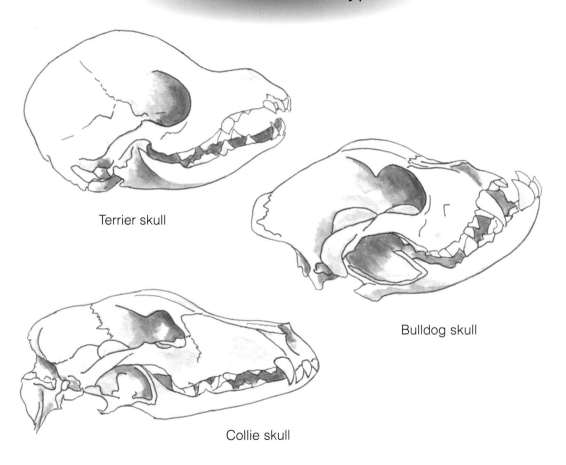

Terrier skull

Bulldog skull

Collie skull

The shape of the canine skull and, to a lesser extent, the size of the skull play a large part in determining the general appearance of a breed. Combined with face shape, fur type and weight, these factors create distinguishing features that enable us to differentiate between breeds.

Teeth

Dogs are predatory, and meat constitutes a large part of their diet. The shape and formation of their teeth reflect this as dogs have the sharp teeth needed for killing prey and chewing tough meat. Dogs have 42 permanent teeth and 28 deciduous teeth. There are four sets of teeth in the canine mouth:

Incisors The incisor teeth are located at the front of the mouth and are used for tearing and shearing food.

Canines The canine teeth are used for holding food while it is being sheared and are located to the rear of the incisors.

Premolars The premolar teeth are located behind the canines and are used for crushing and grinding. Premolars are considered transitional teeth over which food passes during chewing.

Molars The molar teeth are located at the back of the mouth and are used for crushing food, but to a lesser extent than the premolars

◄ Healthy teeth were vital to dogs in the wild, who would soon die once unable to hunt and feed upon the carcass.

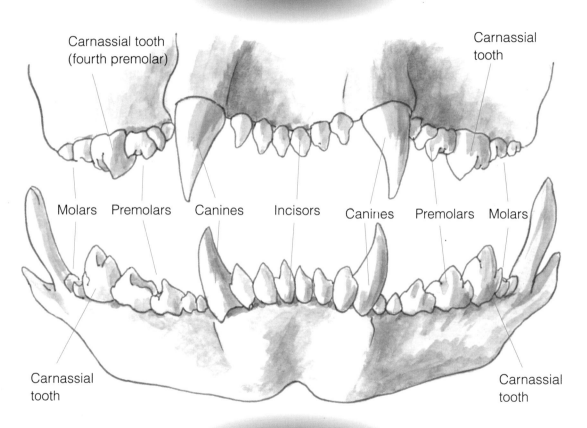

Upper Mandible

Carnassial tooth
(fourth premolar)

Carnassial
tooth

Molars   Premolars   Canines   Incisors   Canines   Premolars   Molars

Carnassial
tooth

Carnassial
tooth

Lower Mandible

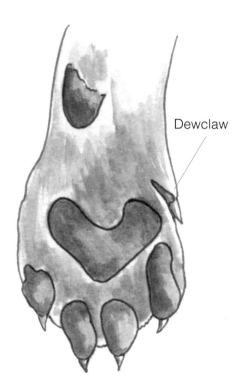

Dewclaw

▲ Dogs sweat through their leathery paw pads.
They usually have a dewclaw on the inside of the
front legs and occasionally on the hind legs.

Dental Health

The overall health of a dog is dependent on the
health of its teeth. In the wild a dog with broken
or unhealthy teeth would soon die from either
starvation or an inability to defend itself,
whichever came first. The modern, domesticated
dog tends not to get enough of the food items
that promote good oral health. In the wild dogs
would eat almost all of any animal they killed –
each part of the carcass would bring its own
benefit. Now that most dogs are fed soft,
processed pet food the friction needed to clean
the teeth is missing. Infected teeth and gums can
quickly lead to toxins being spread through the
digestive system. It is therefore essential that
dogs have healthy teeth.

Nails

In an evolutionary context nails, or claws, were
essential for hunting, feeding and burying – three
things that come to the dog instinctively. Since dogs
use their claws far less in the domestic world it is
important that they are clipped before they become
too long. In the wild the nails would wear down
naturally, but overlong nails can lead to limited mobility
and be painful.

The Senses

Nature has given the dog a set of senses that has equipped it to thrive in the wild, principally sight, hearing and smell. The dog has proven to be a valuable ally to man due to the sophistication of some of its senses. Dogs have been bred for their sight and their scenting ability and all dogs have exceptional hearing. The development of the canine senses has been shaped by nature and evolution, as well as by man.

Any environment that limits a sense tends to promote the development of the other senses. Dogs that evolved in open areas such as desert tend to have strong eyesight to enable them to locate prey from a distance. Dogs that evolved in areas where food prey and predators were able to hide will typically have extremely advanced scenting capabilities. Dogs with strong hearing tend to have evolved in areas where the ability to use sight or scent for protection was limited.

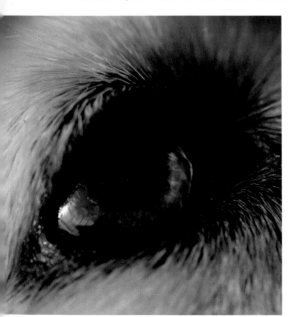

Sight

Almost every breed of dog has keen eyesight. Some have exceptional eyesight, having evolved over time to accommodate the sharpest vision possible. Natural selection dictates that dogs with weak eyesight would not survive as well as dogs that are able to see food

◄　The Afghan Hound is a sight hound, with good peripheral vision, as required by his hunting and living in the mountains of Afghanistan.

sources and predators. The extent to which a breed's sight is developed depends on its role. The shape of a dog's skull also strongly influences its visual ability. Dogs with long, slender heads tend to have better peripheral vision, while dogs with round heads have sharper front-on and long-distance vision.

Scent

One of the most valuable skills a dog has in the working environment is scenting, simply because it is something that humans cannot do for themselves. Comparing the scenting ability of a human and a dog, it is easy to see just how advanced the canine is. If a human can identify a smell as sausages, a dog will be able to identify every ingredient, the chemicals contained therein and the effects that refrigeration and cooking have had on those ingredients. It stands to reason that dogs with large noses have better scenting capabilities, but other physical factors influence this sense as well. A dog with large ears and loose skin around the muzzle will generally be able to retain scent particles near to the nose for

◄ Air-scenting is one of the tools used by the German Shorthaired Pointer to track wounded prey when working as a gun dog.

► The nose, like the paw pads, contains sweat glands. Humans cannot begin to mimic a dog's sense of smell with technology.

longer than a dog with short ears and fur. This is why many scent hounds have thick folds of skin on the face and large, drooping ears.

Hearing

The hearing capabilities of the dog are generally more advanced than our own; however, a dog's hearing deteriorates earlier in life and more rapidly than that of a human. Evolution has influenced the hearing of many dog breeds, particularly those that originally inhabited wooded or grassed areas where vision would have been limited. Dogs have the ability to move their outer ears to pick up on sounds and they can also hear extremely high-frequency noises that are not detected by human ears.

Senses Used to Our Advantage

These three vital senses possessed by the canine are all of use to man, hence why we put the dog to work in so many different environments. A guard dog needs to have excellent hearing in order to alert its master to an intruder; hunting dogs rely on either sight or scent, or in some cases both.

In order for us to exploit the canine senses it has been necessary for us to breed those dogs with the strongest senses in order to protect the bloodlines and gene pools that produced these abilities.

▶ A Siberian Husky gazes attentively, his ears pricked, making the most of his excellent hearing.

Skin and Coat

The general appearance of a dog is influenced largely by its coat. Colouration, length and type of hair are often the only distinguishing features between two otherwise identical breeds. Nature has played its part in developing many varying types of coat and some breeds are noted particularly for the type of coat that they have. The skin of a dog tends to be the same from breed to breed, but there are certain variations and subtle differences that are the result of selective breeding and evolution.

Coat

The coat is the overall combination of fur or hair and the condition and appearance thereof. The health of a dog can be judged by the condition of the coat: a shiny, glossy coat indicates excellent health and good diet; a dull, patchy coat that is lacking lustre points to ill health and a poor diet. The coat of a dog is determined by nature (for example, climate) and sometimes by selective breeding and the working role of the animal.

Fur

Almost all of the world's dogs are covered in fur, with the exception of certain hairless breeds. The fur or hair serves the main purposes of protecting the skin from the elements and keeping the dog warm. There are two

◄ A glossy coat acts a barometer to indicate good health. A dull or patchy coat can indicate malnutrition or ill-health. Curly Coated Retriever.

► Dogs that have been bred for cold climates, such as the Siberian Husky, usually have a thick soft undercoat for insulation.

types of fur found on the coat of a dog: soft undercoat hair, which is commonly found in dogs that evolved in cold countries such as the Siberian Husky; and guard hair, typically stiffer and coarser and there to protect the skin and undercoat from the cold.

Types of coat

Some dogs are double-coated, meaning that they have an abundance of undercoat and guard hair, while other breeds have short, coarse guard hair only. Certain breeds exist in long-coated and short-coated varieties, but this is due more to selective breeding than to evolution. The most common type of coat is short, as most dogs evolved in countries where short hair was necessary. Dogs that were regularly in water tend to have denser, often very curly hair that would have helped to keep them warm when swimming.

Shedding

Shedding is the process by which excess hair is expelled from the coat; this normally happens during the warmer months. Not all dogs shed their hair and Poodles are popular for this reason. Shedding is

◄ The dense, curly coat of the Poodle makes for ideal protection against cold when swimming

normally due to a dog evolving in a location that has extreme climates, such as central Europe. Dogs that evolved in the far north of Europe, such as the Spitz breeds, tend not to shed as much hair as they require a thick coat all year round. Similarly, dogs that evolved in permanently hot countries tend not to shed as much.

Skin

The skin of the dog is rarely seen as it is almost always covered in fur. Some dogs have looser skin, which gives them a wrinkly appearance, while other dogs have noticeably tighter skin, often a result of selective breeding because of the role that dog was intended to play. The skin of a dog is normally pinkish or white in complexion and should be free of dryness and irritation.

▲ Dogs from temperate climates tend to shed their fur most, to deal with extremes of temperature. Chow Chows shed little.

When observing skin types it becomes apparent just how much man has influenced the physical appearance of the dog. The Shar Pei has exceptionally loose skin, which can cause it severe health problems. This has happened because of man's desire for the breed, which was used for fighting, to be able to tolerate being bitten and to be able to move while another dog has a grip.

Colours and Markings

The complex genetics associated with the canine species have created a whole host of interesting and attractive colourings. Many of the colours are referred to in their specificity to dogs, while others are merely standard colours. For every colour, from the jet black of

the Russian Black Terrier to the snow white of the Samoyed, there are a multitude of combinations and mixtures. Different colours and patterns are associated with different breeds and many dog types are defined by the appearance of their coat.

Common Canine Colours

The most common colours found in modern dog breeds are black, white, brown, tan and combinations of these. Some dogs exhibit lighter or darker shades of these colours, depending on breeding and genetics. The colouration of many dogs is due to the presence of other breeds in the bloodline – for example, the Doberman inherited its distinctive black and tan colouration from the Rottweiler. Sometimes cross breeding two pure-bred dogs can result in new, or at least very rare, colourations and patterns. Interestingly a small

number of dogs retain all of the physical attributes of one parent with the exception of colouration, which they inherit from the other. In these cases the dog may look like a pure-bred breed in the 'wrong' colour, but it is in fact a cross-breed. It is rare for this to happen, but some new colours have been developed this way.

Unusual Canine Colours

Shades such as apricot, lemon, chocolate and merle are more rare than the standard blacks and browns, but some dogs are associated strongly with these colourations.

◄ Many breeds of dog have distinctive markings. Labrador Retrievers, however, have a solid-coloured coat: black, yellow or chocolate.

► The light-coloured coat of the Great Pyrenean traditionally allowed it to meld with its flock and surprise predators.

Spaniels, for example, come in a variety of colours, patterns and colour combinations. Some colourations are more unusual than others and occasionally breeders are wary of dogs exhibiting rare colourations as it indicates a deviation from the typical standard.

Canine Patterns and Markings

Aside from colour, dogs can be identified by their markings. The Dalmatian is well known for its spotted coat, which occurs in black and white and, less frequently, liver and white. Some types of Great Dane, notably the Harlequin Great Dane, also exhibit spotted coats.

Brindle, which appears as blended striping of two similar shades, is associated with certain breeds and is a very eye-catching pattern. Staffordshire Bull Terriers often exhibit wonderful brindle coats, as do many hunting hounds.

Patterns such as merle, sable and ticked are often very striking – mixing lighter and darker shades of the same colour or even contrasting colours such as black and white. It is often considered a departure from a breed standard for a dog not to display certain patterns.

◄ Merle colouring results from a mixing of the standard breed colouring, giving attractive paler coat markings.

► The Dalmatian is famous for its spotted coat, similar to that of the Harlequin Great Dane (left) which is harder to achieve in Great Dane litters.

What Do Colours Mean?

Nature often uses colour in order for animals to understand the world and environment around them. While this does not hold true to the same extent in the canine world as it does with, for example, poisonous animals, it still has an effect.

The colour of a dog is caused in the most part by genetics – environment and working role have much less to do with it. However, in certain instances colour is associated directly with behaviour and health. Dogs that are a solid white colour are more prone to skin cancer than other dogs. The colour white is also associated with deafness in many breeds, especially in Boxers. In cases where white is rare for a certain breed, differences in standard behaviour may be present. For example, German Shepherd Dogs are typically a mixture of brown, black or grey, but occasionally all-white German Shepherds are born. The gene that gives the dog this coat of solid white is associated with instances of difficult behaviour and extreme temperament.

▲ The Sable coat of the Shetland Sheepdog can range from pale gold to deep mahogany.

▶ Pure white breeds may be particularly prone to deafness, as with pure white White Boxers.

Canine Terminology

There are many terms and phrases that are dog-specific. In order for the dog to be referenced accurately in terms of form, shape and appearance, it is important to understand the specific names that are used.

Head and Skull Terminology

When discussing the physiology of the canine head, certain terms are used to ensure that descriptions are accurate. Dog heads come in many different shapes and sizes and it is essential, for the purposes of breeding and conformation, that there are sufficiently accurate and descriptive terms.

Brachycephalic The type of skull that is broad with a short muzzle and flat face; for example Pugs (right).
Dolichocephalic A skull that is long and narrow; Greyhounds and Dobermans (left) display this shape.
Flews The flews are the top lips, but this term is used more commonly to describe upper lips that happen to be pendulous and large, as seen on breeds from the Molosser family of dogs.
Mesatacephalic A medium-sized head, both in width and in length.
Bite The way a dog's jaw sits when the mouth is closed; a dog can have a level bite, an under-shot bite or an over-shot bite.
Occiput The highest point at the back of the skull, where the head and neck meet.
Stop A typically depressed area of the face above the muzzle.
Drop ears A description used for large, low-hanging ears, such as those of the Bloodhound or Bassett Hound.

Ear carriage This phrase is used in two contexts: firstly it describes the way the ears of any given breed naturally sit on the head; and secondly it refers to the movement of the dog's ears as it uses them to communicate mood.

Ears set on Dogs' ears are set either on high, on low or on wide.

Ear feather The specific growth of thick fur on the outer ears, as seen in breeds such as Springer Spaniels and Cocker Spaniels.

Prick ears Prick ears stand erect and are set on high; examples include Spitz-type dogs and the German Shepherd Dog.

Body Terminology

When talking about the body of a dog people often refer to body parts and areas in human terms. Although this is applicable in some contexts, the shape of a dog's body and the fact that it is not upright or bipedal means that there are parts that don't exist in the human form, and there are specific terms that refer to these parts.

Similarly, there are terms that are used to differentiate context. When talking about dogs in general it may be acceptable to refer to chest or shoulders. But when talking about the physiology of the canine it is much more appropriate to use the correct terminology, such as brisket and withers.

◀ Drop ears and feathering (longer hairs), on the ears of breeds such as Cocker Spaniel, prevent air circulation, increasing susceptibility to infection.

Brisket The chest, specifically when mention-ing the appearance and shape of the outer chest.

Hock A joint found on the hind leg roughly where the knee would be, although it is more comparable to the heel in function.

Topline The line of the spine as it runs from the neck to the tail.

Dewlap The fold of skin that hangs below the lower jaw; it is more prominent in heavier breeds with looser skin, such as the Bull Mastiff.

Withers The highest point of the dog aside from the head – where the shoulders would be on a human. This is the point to which dogs are typically measured.

Shoulders The shoulders on a dog are located at the front, where the top of the foreleg meets the brisket.

Loin The area around the lower ribs and pelvis, where the genitals are located.

Forequarters Terminology

Due to the fact that the fore-and hind legs look and work differently, it is very important to be able to differentiate between the different parts of the limbs. The front legs bend backwards at the pastern, while the hind legs should not bend.

Foreleg The anatomical term for the front leg, which is formed and functions differently from the hind leg.

Pastern The part of the foreleg where the limb bends above the paw.

Paw The base of the dog's foot.

Paw pad The leathery parts of the sole of the paw.

▶ The drooping jowls found on some heavier breeds, for instance, Bull Mastiff, are known as the 'dewlap'.

Toes Dogs typically have three toes on each foot but sometimes there are four, depending on breeding.

Dewclaw This is considered to be an additional toe, located above the foot, which occurs in some breeds.

Hare foot A foot that has two elongated middle toes; breeds with this feature include the Greyhound and the Borzoi.

Webbed Some dogs, notably those bred for water work such as the Field Spaniel and the Newfoundland, have webbed feet – enabling greater propulsion through the water.

Nails Claws sometimes are referred to as nails or toenails. The term claw is more common when referring to the nails when used all together, in the same way that the human hand is referred to as a fist when all fingers are in use.

Quick Canine toenails contain a blood vessel called the quick; when grooming it is essential not to cut the quick but to trim the nail just below it.

Tail Terminology

Tails can be short, long, well coated and come in many different shapes. There are a handful of terms that are used when referring to the tail of a dog.

Tapered A tail that gets thinner towards the end.

Docked A tail that has had part or most of it removed by a cosmetic or veterinary process.

Screw tail A short, curly tail.

Bob tail A short stumpy tail, as found on the Pembroke Welsh Corgi.

◄ Newfoundland dogs have webbed feet adapted for swimming.

► The stumpy tail of the Pembroke Welsh Corgi is not a result of docking; it has been bred that way.

Coat Terminology

There is a multitude of coats found among the various dog breeds. In most cases simple descriptions are inadequate and it is necessary to use the correct terms when describing a dog's coat.

Corded A coat that grows in such a way that it becomes intertwined; this type of coat is found on the Komondor – a very distinctive-looking herding dog.

Single coat Any coat that lacks an undercoat is single coated.

Double coat Found on dogs from cold climates, a double coat features both underhairs and guard hairs.

Feathered Feathering of a coat occurs at the ears, tail and various other parts of some breeds, such as a Saluki.

Flag This describes long tufts of hair on the tail.

Jacket Dogs with a short coat, such as the Staffordshire Bull Terrier, are described as having a jacket.

Mane This describes the growth of hair around the back of the neck when it is out of proportion with the hair growth on other parts of the body; the Leonberger is a breed with a mane.

Plume A heavily feathered tail carried over the back is described as a plume; the Bichon Frise has a plumed tail.

Stand-off coat This describes the type of coat in which the hairs stick out, almost as if they have been blow-dried.

Topknot The topknot is a tuft of hair on the top of the head, as found on the Afghan Hound.

◄ The Saluki has attractive feathering on the ears and tail.

► The Komondor, traditionally from Hungary, is distinctive for its corded coat, with long twined tassels of fur.

Behaviour

Throughout man's long relationship with the dog an understanding of their emotional, physical and environmental needs has developed. The dog is no longer a wild hunter, but a tame and adaptable companion. Through domestication dogs have become more sensitive to the human environment and, in turn, man has taken a keener interest in the way dogs function and behave. An understanding of the behavioural patterns of these animals is essential for any dog owner, and is particularly useful when deciding which breed to buy.

Intelligence and Psychology

Cognition is a scientifically accepted concept used for measuring the relative intelligence of animals, and the dog has been proved to be one of the most intelligent animals on Earth. Dogs display certain behaviours, such as problem solving and decision making, which mark them out as being particularly intelligent. While intelligence is a broad concept to apply, it is true to say that the dog as a species has a high level of intelligence. The Border Collie is believed to be the most intelligent breed of all.

Learning

In order to learn and develop new skills animals must possess the ability to process information. The dog has the requisite mental capacity for developing and remembering new skills. For example, a dog can be

▶ It is the ability to remember instructions that make even young puppies trainable in a variety of skills.

trained to perform any number of functions in response to a given stimulus. In order to do this, a process called operant conditioning comes into force, by which patterns of association are made between actions and consequences.

Cognition

A dog will associate actions, functions and operants with stimuli and consequences. For example, if a dog puts its paw on a hot surface it will remember that putting its paw in that place results in physical pain and will therefore, if it is wise, not do the same thing again. While it will not understand the concept of either heat or pain, it will make a connection between the action and the consequence. However, if the dog puts its paw on a hot surface while somebody blows a whistle, the dog is just as likely to associate the sound of the whistle with the consequence of pain as it is to associate it with the act of putting its paw on the hot surface. This concept enables us to manipulate the dog's actions through various stimuli.

Instincts

Through the process of evolution, nature has equipped the canine with a set of instincts that have enabled it to survive as a species. Almost all of the instincts we witness in domestic pet dogs are retained from previous generations of wild dogs. While certain instincts may relate to territory,

reproduction, food or dominance, each instinct is inextricably linked back to the survival of the species. Protection of the weak, such as puppies, dominance over inferiors and howling are all instinctive behaviours.

Food

Dogs see all food as their food; this is because nature has taught them to eat whatever they can. Sometimes this instinct will overpower all other stimuli, such as training and distraction. Each dog is governed more strongly by certain instincts, but all instincts relate to survival. Aggression around food is instinctive for some dogs but this may be overridden by the instinct to avoid conflict, which is why some dogs give in if challenged for food.

Reproduction

To enable a species to thrive and survive, the strongest must breed. The female is instinctively driven to mate with the strongest and healthiest male she can find, typically the alpha male in the pack. All males are driven to mate with whichever female they can, in order to continue their bloodline. Nature gave every dog the need to reproduce so that the competition among them would ensure the strongest thrived.

Protection

Instincts such as turning around before lying down, sleeping in a curled up position or puffing out the chest when frightened are all related to the dog's need to

◀ The traditional greeting between dogs, as they sniff each other's rears, is part of the mating ritual.

▶ Dogs' instincts have evolved through the need to survive; consequently a dog might growl if you approach its food bowl.

protect itself. By turning around before settling, a dog is subconsciously ensuring that nothing dangerous is about before it rests. The habit of sleeping in a curled up position is done in order to protect vital organs when vulnerable.

Communication

Dogs communicate in a sophisticated and clear manner. The majority of canine communication is done via body language: eye movement, body shape, ear position and even tail height are all very clear signs that other dogs will easily understand. Barking, growling and howling are used far less frequently as a means of communication than body language. Much of the dog's language is derived from instinct – even puppies display communicative body language within the litter, and this often helps establish pack order.

Aggression

Signs of aggression are more subtle than people realize. Before a dog resorts to growling or biting, it will have given many warning signs. Holding its gaze, licking its lips and holding its tail high outwards are all signs that a dog is feeling threatened. The main instinct when feeling threatened is to avoid violence; this is done by communicating an intention to act if and when called for.

◄ Dogs' tails are vital in communicating with other dogs; a tail sticking straight out indicates aggression. A dog may also attempt to out-stare another dog to establish dominance.

Fear

If a dog is scared it may display this in a number of possible ways. Some dogs will become submissive, exposing their stomach and therefore their vital organs in an act that shows that they are not a threat. Other dogs will become defensive and may bark, growl or bare their teeth. Barking is a language in and of itself – each type of bark has its own meaning: loud, constantly repeated barks signal the intention to make an aggressive move; high-pitched, intermittent barking is a sign of fear but with less intention of acting in defence.

Dominance

Dogs need to know who is the more dominant. A submissive dog will never attempt to dominate a more superior dog. Dominance is communicated through posture, head position, body language and general actions. A dominant dog may indicate its superiority by pushing past an inferior dog or may do so by holding the gaze of another dog until the inferior animal looks away.

Breed Differences and Personality Types

Personality differs from dog to dog, but it differs even more so from breed to breed. Certain breeds are associated with certain types of behaviour and personality, and these attributes can be traced back to the working roles of that particular breed. In some cases dogs demonstrate atypical personality attributes for their breed. All dogs share some very important personality traits, such as a drive to eat, reproduce and protect, but other attributes are more breed specific.

Intelligence

Intelligence is associated with working pastoral and herding breeds such as the Border Collie and German Shepherd. Due to the breeding stock that was initially used and the type of work the dogs are used to doing, any dog that has a history of droving or herding will be of above-average intelligence.

Aggression

Aggression is present in all breeds, as it is linked to the survival instinct, but some dogs are more prone to becoming aggressive more easily. These tend to be breeds that were bred originally for guarding or for fighting as their ancestors were selected especially because of their propensity for aggression.

Loyalty

Almost every breed is inherently loyal, with the possible exception of a few breeds that are used for lone hunting. Hound breeds are likely to be more loyal than most dogs, often to the exclusion of other family members. The Greyhound is known for its devotion; this is because of the natural inclination the dog has to form a partnership with a master, due to its working origins.

Tenacity

Tenacity, manifested either in play or work, is most prevalent in terrier breeds. Terriers were required to be hard, energetic workers, so only the ones with the right skills were used for breeding, meaning that the terriers of today typically display a great deal of tenacity and vigour.

▶ Border Collies are famed for their intelligence.

Getting ready for your
Dog

Owning a Dog

Dog ownership is a big commitment. There are hundreds of thousands of dogs in rescue shelters around the world because people did not do their research before acquiring a dog. Owning a dog is not just about picking a cute pup and taking it home; a responsible dog owner will consider a whole host of factors before making the decision to buy. The size of your home, the people in your family (whether you have children, for example), the amount of free time you have and even the nature of your work can have a large influence on your suitability as a dog owner.

Points to Consider

Sharing your life with a dog is fulfilling, rewarding and fun. But good dog ownership starts even before you choose a breed. A good dog owner will research what type of dog they are best equipped to look after. Dogs have differing requirements and personalities – some dogs require lots of exercise, lots of food and lots of space, others are more laid back and prefer a quiet life. Knowing what you can realistically offer a dog in terms of care is the first step in finding the right dog for you. A good dog owner will also be confident that they can afford the veterinary bills, food and grooming costs associated with dog ownership over the animal's entire lifetime.

Puppy or Adult?

The joy of bringing home a new puppy is hard to match. But getting an older dog has many advantages too. In most cases older dogs are house-trained, and have a history that enables new dog owners to make more

informed choices regarding suitability. With so many older dogs in rescue centres there is a wide choice of breeds and ages for prospective dog owners to choose from, and the cost is often much lower than that of buying a puppy. In many cases dogs at rescue centres are 'free to a good home'.

Finding Your Dog

There are numerous ways a potential dog owner can go about finding the right dog for them, but you have to be sure that you are properly equipped in terms of time, space, lifestyle and funds before beginning the search. It is easier to decide that you are not quite ready for dog ownership prior to seeing lots of adorable pups. Once the decision is made to get a dog, it is important to find out what breed, sex, age and type will suit you.

Breeder

Although you may be able to purchase a puppy from a pet shop, buying directly from a breeder can have many benefits. A breeder is often enthusiastic about the breed he or she specializes in and will be prepared to give plenty of advice. If you buy a dog from a breeder, he or she should be able to show you the puppies with their mother. This will allow you to see how each litter member interacts, thus enabling you to pick the one with the personality that best complements your situation.

◄ Do proper research into which breed would suit you, before visiting an adorable litter that will be hard to resist.

Breeders typically breed for the love of the dog, rather than for money, so do not be surprised if the breeder you visit bases his or her operations at home. The breeder may also ask for your references, and some insist on visiting potential homes. Make sure you ask a lot of questions, and do not select a dog until you are absolutely sure.

Rescue Centre or Shelter

Some people prefer to get their dog from a shelter or rescue centre. These places are home to many different types of dogs, of varying breeds, ages and backgrounds. Sadly, some may have been abandoned or mistreated, so seek advice from the staff on which dogs may be more challenging.

There will also be a good number of older dogs looking for a home; typically these will be house-trained and less active than pups.

Before handing over a dog, all good shelters will require a visit to your home to ensure that your set-up is suitable. Also, the better – often breed-specific – rescue homes usually take a profile of prospective owners, and then match a specific dog to you, in order to avoid 'returns' as much as possible.

▲ Buying a puppy is an important decision; sadly too many dogs end up in rescue centres, such as Battersea Dogs Home.

From a Friend

You may choose to take a puppy from a dog with which you are already familiar. The advantage of this is that you will know the parent dogs and can make a better judgement of how the puppy is likely to turn out.

Accommodation

There are a handful of important things to do before you are ready to receive your dog. These issues relate to health, safety and good animal husbandry and care. Speaking to the breeder and other experienced dog owners is a good step. It is essential to decide before receiving a dog into your home where your dog will sleep, what access it will have to other parts of the house and how it will be transported.

First Things First

There are a number of things to consider before bringing a dog into your life. Research and planning are essential to providing good care for your dog; speak to others and be prepared to respond to your pet's individual needs.

Health

When choosing a dog, especially a pure-bred, you should endeavour to get as much information relating to health as possible. Hip scores (points-based scores indicating the risk or levels of hip dysplasia, achieved by

◄ Many pure bred dogs have tendencies to a health weakness of some sort or other; Bulldogs are prone to heart disease.

assessing radiographs of the dog's hips) and other health information should be readily available from the breeder. Also be aware of breed-specific problems, such as heart complaints in Bulldogs and skin problems in Bull Mastiffs.

It is essential to research the vets in your area – knowing where the nearest one is will be useful but ensure that you research all of your options. Veterinary prices and services vary greatly, so ensure that you find a vet with whom you are comfortable. You will need a vet to administer vaccinations if you are bringing home a puppy.

Safety

By the time you bring home your dog you should be aware of the likely behaviour of the breed. Being equipped with this information will enable you to make judgements pertaining to safety. Removing any potential hazards from the immediate vicinity is essential. Be aware of which items and areas the new dog is showing an interest in. Many dogs like to investigate fireplaces because of the smells – obviously this is a bad habit for the dog to get into.

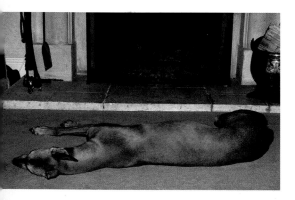

Your Dog's Environment

Prior to bringing your new dog home it is essential to ensure that your house or flat is dog- or puppy-friendly. This means that it must be safe, comfortable and conducive to good mental health. Common sense dictates

◄ Dogs often enjoy the warmth of a fire, choosing prime position.
A fire guard is essential with a curious pup.

many of the necessary steps in preparing your home, but do seek advice from other dog owners. It is not essential that all dogs have access to a large garden, but it must be possible for dogs to be given fresh air, exercise and stimulation regularly. Dogs need to relieve themselves several times a day. Thus, for example, if you go out to work all day, you must take your dog out in the morning before you leave, as soon as you return home, and again before bed-time. During the day it should be let out by someone, or perhaps have access to outdoors via a dog-flap. But, ideally a dog is never left alone all day.

Bed or Sleeping Area

For it to be happy the dog must have an area of the home that it can call its own. This is typically a dog bed or basket located in a quiet part of the house. The area must be clean, preferably near to an outside door to aid toilet training and free from hazardous objects such as potentially poisonous plants. Your dog must feel safe and secure in this area.

Out-of-bounds Areas

Deciding before its arrival in the home where the dog is allowed to go and making sure that this can be enforced is essential. Some people prefer to give their dog a free reign, but it is wise to limit a dog's access to areas such as the garage, stairs, outhouses and sheds and any area used to store tools. A child safety gate is a good method of restricting access to certain parts of the home.

▶ The boundaries of your garden should be dog-proof, to prevent your dog straying or getting injured by traffic. These dogs could easily squeeze or dig under this gate if they really wanted. It should have some strong plastic-coated mesh attached to the bottom.

Any area where the dog could feasibly escape should be classed as out-of-bounds. Broken fences, low walls and open driveways should be rendered inaccessible for a dog. Use discouragement training methods to ensure that the dog is not tempted to wander out of the garden.

The Feeding Area

The area where the dog is fed must be clean and free from distractions. Many dogs are territorial and protective when eating, so any area that is busy, such as the kitchen, is not necessarily suitable as a dog-feeding area.

Nature has taught dogs to keep their immediate environment, known as the den, clean and tidy. It is essential when house-training a dog that it is not forced or encouraged to go to the toilet in or near the area where it sleeps and eats. This is counter-instinctive and will cause distress to a dog, especially a brood bitch.

A Dog-friendly Home

A dog's home needs to be secure, clean and safe. Sharp corners and slippery surfaces are potentially hazardous for a dog. Large breeds often struggle to keep their footing across polished or smooth surfaces; however, many dog owners prefer smooth surfaces

◄ Large breeds can find smooth floor surfaces, such as wood or lino, slippery. Rugs help to prevent their paws sliding.

such as wood or tiles for ease of cleaning. Putting down a rug on a slippery floor is a good way of getting around this problem. The corners of low work units are difficult to avoid, but discouraging your dog from encountering such hazards can be achieved by placing his bed away from such areas.

A Dog-friendly Garden

Ponds and pools must be dog-safe. Dogs may have no difficulty jumping into the water, but getting out if the sides are steep is difficult. Never leave a dog unsupervised in or near water and use training to discourage your dog from exploring water features. A garden should be free from other hazards such as poisonous vegetation and gravel, particularly loose-pack gravel that can become stuck in between a dog's paw pads, leading to infection and discomfort. Ensure that your garden takes into account a dog's inquisitive nature.

Travelling and Boarding

Dog ownership, being the large commitment that it is, requires the owner to make many major lifestyle choices (such as holiday destination and even the type of car they drive) with the needs of their pet in mind. Many people choose to holiday domestically so that they can bring their dog along; others choose to board their dog while they are away. There are numerous factors to consider that affect both choices and sufficient research and planning is essential.

▶ While dogs are naturally good swimmers, care must be taken near pools and ponds; steep sides are difficult to scrabble out of.

Travelling

Travelling with a dog can be very easy. It is necessary to provide a safe and secure place in the car so that the dog is restrained. Crates, special canine car seats or improvised boot spaces, provided they are safe, are all popular means of transporting a dog. Large breeds offer more problems when travelling, as often they do not fit comfortably into crates.

It is a good idea to introduce your dog to the car prior to making that first journey. This ensures that the dog is familiar with the environment before undergoing the new and highly stimulating experience of car travel. Taking some treats along is also advisable; as is taking some familiar bedding that will smell like their 'territory'.

Boarding

Sometimes it is necessary to put a dog into boarding accommodation. Many dog owners try to avoid this scenario, but in reality a boarding kennel is often preferable to leaving a dog with an inexperienced friend or relative.

Ensure that you speak to, meet and inspect the premises of any boarding-kennel owner or manager before committing your dog to their care. Following one's instincts with regards to boarding kennels is a good idea: if a place does not feel right then find somewhere else. It is absolutely essential that the boarding staff are aware of any medical and feeding requirements your dog may have.

Essential Equipment

Becoming a dog owner brings with it an obligation to invest in essential items to provide good animal care. Toys, grooming tools, feeding paraphernalia and other items – as well as the dog food itself – do not come cheap, so it is a good idea to budget for these items before committing to bringing a dog into your home. Depending on the breed of your dog certain specialist items may be necessary, such as sophisticated grooming items or a special harness; researching which items will be needed is essential.

Grooming

Some dogs require far less grooming than others, but it is important for all dogs to be groomed, even if it is just a quick comb through of the coat to remove dead skin, dirt and excess hairs. Depending on the level of grooming, the equipment can be relatively cheap or fairly expensive.

Coat The coat may be groomed with a slicker brush or a stiff metal comb depending on coat type.

Cleanliness It is important to bathe dogs, but not too regularly. Special shampoo and conditioners are available.

Claws Trimming the claws can be done at home or by a vet or groomer. Normally a pair of standard dog nail

clippers is sufficient. It is essential you know what you are doing, and do not cut into the quick of the dog's claws.

Feeding Equipment

The environment in which a dog feeds must be clean and free from hazards. It is always best to invest in good-quality items that your dog will come to associate with feeding time.

Metal food and water bowl A metal food bowl is easy to clean, durable and lightweight. There must be a separate bowl for water and this must be kept topped up with fresh, clean water throughout the day.

Ceramic food bowl Ceramic bowls are heavier and therefore stay in place when the dog is eating from them. Larger dogs need heavier bowls otherwise they can end up tipping food all over the floor and creating a hazard. Ceramic food bowls are more difficult to clean than metal. Due to a dog's extremely sensitive nose any food residue that is decaying on a ceramic bowl can cause a dog to be put of its food, so you must double-check that you have cleaned it thoroughly.

Food dispenser Keeping a dog's food fresh and free from bugs and insects is essential. Vermin are often attracted to pet food if it is left in a bag in the garage. A plastic, closable food dispenser keeps the food fresh and untainted.

▶ Metal food bowls are hygienic and unbreakable. But if you have a medium or large-size dog, it is liable to tip over such lightweight bowls.

▲ An identity tag on a collar is very useful should your
dog go missing. Keep a check, however, as the
tags can come off.

Other Essential Equipment

Apart from grooming and feeding equipment there
are other items that will be vital for your dog's safety
and happiness.

Collar and lead These come in many styles and
designs. Large and strong breeds may be better suited
to a harness, which enables more control. A retractable
lead is good for giving a run to a dog that cannot be
trusted off the lead. Seek advice from a trusted seller or
vet, as some collars are not suitable for some breeds
and some can be dangerous.

Identity All dogs should carry some form of
identification in case they go missing. A simple name-
tag attached to the collar is useful, provided that the
details are up-to-date. Alternatively, many people favour
having a microchip implanted into the dog's skin. This contains all of the information required should a
dog be found, which is read by a scanner and traced back to the owner. The benefit of this is that it
cannot fall off.

Toys Money spent on toys and training equipment should be budgeted for. Dogs require a number of
toys that stimulate them in different ways to prevent boredom. Investing in good-quality, durable toys is
more economical over time.

Toys that are designed to reward the dog, such as those that contain food, are good for keeping the dog
entertained. A ball is a popular toy, but some dogs will simply chew it rather than fetch it.

Caring for your
Dog

Puppy Care

Caring for a newborn puppy is not something that an untrained and inexperienced person should attempt to do. Puppies should never be separated from their mother before eight weeks after birth. The mother is the best source of food, protection and nurturing that the puppy can have. It is counter-productive to remove the puppy from the mother unless due to illness or the mother otherwise being unable to care for the litter, in which case hand rearing may be necessary.

Feeding

For the first weeks of their life puppies suckle at the mother's teat. This is their only source of food at this time and they get all of the nutrients they need from the mother's milk. Newborn and very young puppies do not have teeth. This is because their bodies are not able to tolerate solid food and also because it would cause pain to the nursing bitch.

It is important that a puppy is not weaned from its mother too soon, that is, before six weeks. In order to wean the puppy it is essential to allow it to come off the teat in its own time. Allowing it access to, but not forcing it to eat its mother's solid meals is a suitable method of encouraging the pup to wean. Dogs may also take small amounts of water, as well as mother's milk during the weaning process.

▶ Puppies are born without teeth and for the first weeks should solely drink their mother's milk

Hand Rearing

When caring for a young pup in a domestic situation it is essential that the owner fulfils the role of hunter-gatherer. Providing suitable puppy food and formula is essential. Puppies grow extremely quickly and their nutritional needs change rapidly.

The best way to judge the success of hand rearing a puppy is to observe the young dog's condition, behaviour and energy levels. If it attempts to suckle continually this can be a sign that it is not getting sufficient sustenance from its mother and therefore will need supplementing with other food.

Vets

Vets are a valuable source of information, advice and guidance for owners of young puppies. They are on hand, if required, to monitor the growth and progress of the pup. Weighing the puppy and checking its responses to certain stimuli will give a good indication of general health and well-being. The vet will also administer vaccinations for the puppy that protect against harmful diseases such as parvovirus, distemper and leptospirosis. He or she will also treat the puppy for worms and other parasites. Be sure to keep an up-to-date record of the vaccinations that your puppy has

► Take your puppy to the vet for its routine checks and vaccinations and have it weighed to ensure that it is growing healthily.

received, and do not let the dog out to mix with other dogs until all vaccinations are completed.

Setting-up Home

When puppies are removed from the litter and the mother they can become distressed and disorientated. It is essential that the pup's progress is monitored during this stage. One way of making the transition from being in a litter to being in a new and unfamiliar home is to ensure that your own home provides adequate warmth, security, peace and privacy for the puppy to become accustomed to its new environment.

In the wild puppies are raised in a den. Mimicking a den environment will, to a certain extent, help the puppies accept their new surroundings. Some puppies will make the transition seamlessly and will investigate the new smells and sights of your home with interest. Other puppies will be a little more timid. Whichever way it happens, all puppies will need a clean, warm and comfortable area to call their own in which they can sleep.

> ▶ Some puppies may be timid at first, whilst others are more
> confident. Regardless of this all puppies will need a clean and safe
> area of their own where they can sleep.

Training and Exercise

For a dog to be happy in the domestic environment it needs to be secure of the boundaries and rules that limit behaviour. This is why obedience- and house-training are essential. Training can begin in earnest when the puppy is brought home, but this should involve encouraging the puppy to do the right thing, rather than attempting to teach it to obey commands. The best way to aid training is to begin as you mean to go on – consistency is the key.

Early Learning and Exercise

Probably the first thing that owners will be keen to teach their puppy is knowing where and when to go to the toilet. Patience, a good routine and a balance of discipline and reward should make this and any

other learning process reasonably straightforward. Letting your dog exercise through play and by taking it for regular walks will also aid training and obedience.

Toilet Training

Due to their young age and limited capacity for self-control, puppies will have accidents and go to the toilet

▶ When house-training your puppy it is vital to be calm and consistent and to reward him for going in the correct place.

in the wrong place. The key is not to make a fuss. Putting down newspaper (ensuring it is not close to where the puppy eats or sleeps) should encourage the dog to go in the same place.

It will be necessary on the first few occasions to place the pup on the paper when it is exhibiting the signs of needing to relieve itself. These signs may include sniffing at a door, turning in circles, whining or sniffing the ground. If you suspect the pup needs to go, gently and without excitement guide it to the

newspaper. When the puppy toilets appropriately it should be rewarded. Never rub a dog's nose in the mess if it accidentally goes in the wrong place. This is cruel and does nothing to encourage appropriate toileting.

Routine

Establishing a solid routine is essential to help the puppy adapt to domestic life. Planning for the dog to go to the toilet after waking up and after eating is important, as it increases the chances of it going in the right place.

Letting the dog outside after eating is important, but this should wait until the dog is ready to go outside. Encouraging the dog to exercise may not be necessary at first, as puppies tend to be full of energy for short periods of time, during which they will romp and play until exhaustion.

▶ Puppies are naturally inquisitive and full of play – they will happily scamper about exercising themselves. Parson Russell Terrier puppies.

Rewards

Rewarding a dog's good behaviour is far more effective than punishing bad behaviour. Should the dog misbehave, putting it in its basket or removing a toy tends to be enough. Praise, food and play are all rewarding to dogs, and as such can be used as encouragement during basic training.

Discipline

It is very simple to discipline a dog. Provided that the discipline is even-handed, fair and consistent the dog will learn quickly. By judging what motivates a particular dog it is possible to find the most effective method of discipline. Some dogs respond more to noise, others to sensation such as being pulled gently, for example if they are pulling on the lead. If the dog does something wrong, issue the correction, whether it is in the form of a verbal command such as 'No', a gentle smack on the rump or an aural stimulus, such as whistle or clicker, in a timely and clear fashion. Punishing a dog too long after the deed is ineffective and confusing.

Walking and Play

Puppies will play instinctively – it is how they interact with other puppies in the litter. Walking on a lead, however, is counter-instinctive and therefore needs training and encouragement. Start the process by letting the dog become familiar with the lead; then, on a loose lead,

◄ Puppies are very responsive to your displeasure; be consistent and calm when admonishing them.

► Rewarding a dog's good behaviour is one of the most effective ways to train them.

allow the dog to wander around. Gently guide it back if it wanders too far, while issuing the 'heel' command. As the puppy becomes used to the lead gradually shorten it until you have complete control over the dog. Combine walking on the lead with general obedience training.

Obedience and Further Training

Obedience is the cornerstone of the dog's history of co-operation with man. Without obedience dogs would not have performed any of the valuable functions we needed them to. Dogs are driven by instinct and environment; some of the things we ask them to do are counter-instinctive, such as sitting, which is why we need to train them to do so. Establishing the favour and co-operation of a dog takes time and patience, but is very rewarding.

The 'Sit' Command

The 'sit' command is probably the first command a dog can master. It is easily achieved through a combination of positive reinforcement and encouragement. Teaching a dog to sit should be done in a calm and distraction-free environment.

Capturing the dog's attention is the most important thing to do. Follow this by repeating the 'sit' command while encouraging the dog to sit. This can be done by

◄ Holding a treat in your hand when encouraging your dog to sit will help to keep its attention!

standing in a position where it is more comfortable for the dog to sit in order to see, perhaps by leaning over the dog, or by gently pushing the rump to the ground. Once the dog hits the sit position issue praise and reward to the dog so that it associates its action with the positive consequence. Also ensure that it associates your command with the action.

The 'Down' Command

Once you have mastered the 'sit' command you can move on to the 'down' command. A clever way of achieving this command is by placing a treat in a place where the dog needs to lay down to get it, perhaps under your legs if you are sitting on the ground. The dog will be focused on the treat, but as it attempts to get the treat issue the 'down' command. As soon as it hits the floor let it have the treat.

Controlling Bad Behaviour

Many of the canine's natural instincts are not suited to the domestic environment. Digging and howling, for example, may have served the dog well in the wild but are problematic for dogs living alongside humans. Much bad behaviour associated with domestic dogs is not instinctive but rather the result of the dog pushing its luck to see how far it can go before being corrected. It is often linked to food and access to mates.

▶ By consistent repetition of an instruction you can train your dog so that is understands, for instance, not to sit on the sofa.

Bad Habits

Bad canine habits, such as climbing on furniture or scratching at the door, can easily be controlled. Simply ensure that the dog understands that each time it performs such an action there will be a negative consequence. For practical reasons, it is always preferable that the negative consequence is your voice issuing the 'No' command.

Inappropriate Behaviour

Actions such as jumping up at people, incessant barking and digging are inappropriate and can lead to wider problems if left uncorrected. Discouragement and prevention are preferable to punishment. Manufacturing a situation in which a dog is not tempted to misbehave is a good way of rewarding positive behaviour rather than punishing bad behaviour. Consistency is the key to disrupting bad behaviour patterns. If something is unacceptable it should be unacceptable at all times. Dogs will become confused if they get away with an action in one situation but are punished for it in another.

Aggression

All dogs are capable of acting aggressively, which is why it is essential to correct and discourage such behaviour. The dog should understand its place in the pack or family and therefore should not feel the need to act aggressively. It is essential that you respond to aggression confidently, but not aggressively, as this can exacerbate the situation.

◄ The dog on the right is displaying body-language signals typical of aggression, with bared teeth, lowered head and raised rump.

Feeding

The dog has evolved into a fairly adaptable eater. In the wild dogs would hunt and kill their prey, but in the domestic environment their food is often bought at the local shop. Despite this the nutritional needs of the canine have not changed. The main part of the diet is meat, with cereals, vegetation, fish, some dairy and roughage also required. The food may be all natural or commercial, served in one portion or throughout the day.

Nutritional Needs

It is essential for a dog owner to provide a balanced and nutritional diet for their pet. There are a number of components that should always be present, as well as a few that should be avoided at all costs.

Protein Dogs receive protein through foods such as chicken and meat.

Fat Fat is an essential part of the canine diet, especially for puppies. Meat and fish are good sources of fat.

Calcium Eggs and milk are a good source of calcium.

Fibre Brown rice and oats contain fibre.

Vitamins Parsley and seaweed are good sources of vitamins A, C and E.

Harmful food Grapes, raisins and chocolate are all harmful to dogs.

Feeding Techniques

The technique by which an owner delivers the right nutrients to a dog often depends on the breed, the role and the age of the dog. Other considerations are the dog's diet, health requirements and personality.

Regular Meals

Most owners prefer to feed their dogs at regular intervals. This enables the owner to control more closely the exact intake of nutrients throughout the day, as well as ensuring that the dog has something to look forward to.

One Meal

Some dogs receive just one meal a day, typically in the evening. This is usually quite a large portion, depending on the breed, and contains all of the daily recommended vitamins and nutrients. The practice of feeding one meal per day is suitable for dogs with high energy levels and for dogs that work.

Comfort

If you have a large or tall dog such as a Great Dane, or any of the larger hounds, it will be more comfortable for them – and will ease digestion – if their food bowl is placed on a small shelf or stool, so that they do not have to stoop.

More than One Dog

Dogs are instinctively competitive over food. So if you have more than one dog it is important to give each dog the same, and always separate, feeding spot. Separate dogs with a child gate, or by placing them in different rooms if necessary.

Free Feeding

Working dogs are often given a carcass or lump of meat to gorge on. This is analogous to the way dogs feed in the wild.

Food Types

Depending on breed, activity level, age and owner preference, there are many types of food a dog can eat. Some dogs have special dietary requirements, but most are adaptable and will eat whatever is put down for them. Some owners prefer to stick to a natural diet, which tends to involve more preparation and expense, while others prefer to give a commercial diet that is cheaper and more convenient.

Complete Food

Often marketed as meals, commercially available complete food is designed to deliver all of the required nutrients; there is no need for supplements such as biscuits or kibble. Complete food is typically packaged in a can or sachet and is moist, although dry food with meat in it is also classed as 'complete'.

Dry Food

Dry food is designed to be complementary to other food types, such as meat. It is normally in the form of a biscuit and is good for friction, which helps to clean the teeth of the dog. Feeding a meat and mixer diet, such as tripe or offal and dry food, is now less common, as people find complete food more convenient.

Fresh Food

Meat and vegetables mixed with some dry food is a popular fresh produce meal for domestic dogs. This is typically a more messy and expensive method of feeding, but in general is more appealing to the dog.

Raw Food

Raw meat, while being messy and inconvenient, is very appealing to a dog and contains many enzymes that are valuable to aid digestion in dogs. Raw dog meat often comes in the form of butchers' scraps.

Grooming

Grooming is essential to your dog's overall health and well-being. Parasitic infestations and tangled fur are extremely distressing and unpleasant for dogs; this scenario is easily avoided with regular and thorough grooming. Long-haired breeds obviously require more grooming than short-haired breeds, but a basic level of grooming, with good-quality, suitable tools, is required by all dogs. Grooming is also a good way for a dog owner to bond with their pet.

Grooming Kit

There are some items that are essential equipment for grooming and others that are optional, depending on the type of dog or preference of the owner.

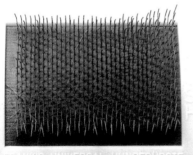

Slicker brush Used for brushing out dirt and tangles from a dog's fur. Not necessary for use on short-haired dogs.

Rubber brush A rubber-bristled brush for use on short-haired coats, to loosen dead hair and surface dirt.

Clippers Used for trimming the nails. If a dog owner is unsure of how to clip the nails they can take the dog to a vet or a professional groomer.

► The slicker brush is useful for removing tangles, particularly from tails and from breeds with longer, finer coats.

Metal comb Used for removing dirt and loose hair from the coat; it is especially useful for short-haired breeds.

Shedder Used to remove loose and dead hair from a dog that is shedding its coat; it can be used throughout the year.

Shampoos Specially formulated shampoos are available for dogs; these are mild and do not sting the eyes but are sufficiently strong to clean the fur.

Sprays Some people like to use specially formulated dog grooming spray, which can leave a dog's coat looking shiny and smelling nice.

Grooming glove It enables the owner to remove stray hair and dirt simply by stroking the dog.

Scissors Some dogs will require their coat to be trimmed quite regularly to avoid matting and tangling.

Massage tools Some dog owners like to massage their dog's body during grooming; this enables the dog to relax and also improves circulation. Massage tools come in many different forms, ranging from a massage brush, which also removes dead hair, to electrically powered massage tools that vibrate.

Grooming Process

The grooming process can be long and drawn out or short and sweet, depending on the breed and the style desired by the owner. Most dog owners prefer to groom their pets in a manner that is traditional, but some people are keen to add a little style to their dog's appearance by using accessories, such as bows and ribbons. Grooming encompasses everything from clipping nails to trimming hair, bathing and cleaning out the ears.

The Coat

All dogs require their coat to be combed clean and made free of tangles and knots. Start with a rubber brush on short-haired dogs. On longer-haired dogs, starting with a slicker brush, you should run the tool gently across the dog's coat, being careful not to tug at any knots or matted areas. Should you find any tangles, common on the belly and at the back of the hind legs in some long-haired breeds, gently tease them out.

Getting the dog used to being groomed and touched frequently is essential to making regular grooming quick and painless.

It is important to bear in mind that long-haired dogs, such as Afghans and Pekinese, require virtually daily grooming – or at least regular clipping to keep to keep the coat at a more manegeable length. And with many medium-coated dogs, such as all the spaniels, sheepdogs and Tibetan Terriers, you need to groom at least weekly. If your dog has been out in grass or fields, you need to check or groom every time to remove burrs or furzes.

Bathing

Dogs should not be bathed too frequently, as this can deplete essential oils in their coat. It is good practice to bathe the dog three or four times a year, depending on the breed and how dirty it gets. After bathing a dog it makes sense also to towel-dry the coat and trim it, if needed, in that order. Never attempt to trim a dirty coat.

Nails

If a dog's nails are left to grow too long they can cause the dog severe discomfort, affect its gait and lead to painful scratches for the owner. If you are unsure of your ability to clip the nails properly, get a professional groomer or vet to do it. In some cases dogs need to be sedated in order for them to allow their nails to be clipped.

◄ Your dog's claws will need clipping as they are unlikely to get sufficient wear to keep them short enough.

► You can learn to clip your dog's nails yourself, or ask the vet or a professional groomer.

Health

It is inevitable that dogs are not going to be in good health all of the time.
However, a balanced diet, lots of exercise, a clean living environment and regular
health checks will go a long way towards keeping a dog healthy. Certain breeds,
due to selective breeding, are prone to specific health problems. It is important to
be able to judge a dog's health and to spot potential problems before they become
very serious, especially when the dog is older and more prone to ailments.

A Healthy Dog

Dogs are incapable of expressing directly that they feel unwell. An owner may notice their dog being a
little off-colour, but by the time a dog allows illness to prevent it from acting normally it can be too late.

However, there are ways of assessing the overall health
of a dog that will enable an owner to become aware of
any slight changes.

Appearance

The way a dog looks is a good indicator of health. The
coat should be full and glossy, not dull and patchy. The

◄ Good diet and exercise will help to maintain your dog's well-being.
As ever, prevention is better than cure. German Shorthaired Pointer.

eyes should be bright, never discoloured. The general behaviour of a dog may change due to illness: lower energy levels or a loss of appetite are telltale signs that there is something wrong. Inspecting a dog's stool if you are worried about illness is another good way to clarify your suspicions; anything out of the ordinary should be referred to a vet.

Routine Health Care

It is good practice to visit the vet for a regular check-up (annual or six-monthly check-ups are the norm for healthy dogs), so that he or she can assess whether the dog is showing any signs of illness. Performing a health check at home, perhaps while grooming, enables you to act quickly in the case of illness. Check the coat condition, teeth and gums, inside their ears and do a thorough hand-pass over the dog, checking for lumps or tenderness. Strange-smelling breath, loss of weight or appetite, loss of energy, a dry nose or aggression are all potential signs of illness or disease.

Canine Ailments

Dogs are susceptible to certain viruses and diseases. Many diseases, such as cancer, are common across all breeds, but other conditions are peculiar to a breed or size of dog. Due to the process of selective breeding the gene pool used for dog breeding is relatively small. This

◄ Routine vaccinations, worming and health checks will help to keep your dog in good health and catch serious ailments early on.

► The parvovirus is a serious illness but your dog can be vaccinated against infection. Black and tan dogs, such as Dobermans, are particularly suseptible to it.

is because breeders wish to magnify and improve on desirable elements of appearance. Unfortunately this process does not give the species an adequate chance to rid itself of genetic disorders.

Acquired Conditions

As with humans, there are some illnesses and viruses that dogs can catch, either from other dogs or from the atmosphere. There are many vaccinations that prevent against the more common viruses, but if vaccinations are not kept up-to-date these viruses can spread quickly among dogs, particularly those that live in close proximity to one another.

Parvovirus This is an extremely contagious and serious virus that will affect either the heart and cardiovascular system or the intestines, depending on the strain. The symptoms include vomiting, diarrhoea, fever and lethargy. It is not curable but it can be treated. Victims typically suffer dehydration, which can lead to other complications. Puppies are particularly prone to the virus but are usually vaccinated against it. Black-and-tan breeds, such as Rottweilers and Dobermans, are prone to parvovirus.

Cancer Any dog breed is prone to cancer, but some breeds are more susceptible to certain types of cancer than others. Dogs with solid white colouring are particularly prone, especially to skin cancer. Since dogs are unable to tell us if they discover a lump or unusual growth it is essential that owners perform regular health checks (as described earlier) to ensure that

▶ If you feel a lump on your dog, it is worth getting the vet to check whether it is malignant or harmless.

any causes for concern can be picked up on immediately. Diet can contribute to cancer-risk in dogs: those with poor diet and dogs that are overweight may be more prone to developing various cancers.

Distemper This is a virus that affects puppies and, to a lesser extent, mature dogs. The virus cannot be cured but the symptoms can be treated with swift veterinary attention; symptoms include dull eye colour, weight loss, fever and vomiting.

Leptospirosis Transmitted through contact with infected urine, this disease is zoonotic – meaning it can be passed between species. It affects the liver and kidneys and can be very serious if left untreated; treatment does not always work due to its complexity. Only some of the strains can be vaccinated against.

Epilepsy Any breed can suffer from epilepsy, which causes seizures and neural disruption. Once the condition is diagnosed, vets may prescribe medication. Owners should take care to be prepared to deal with their dog and prevent it from injuring itself during a seizure. Quite often the dog will recover by itself from a seizure, but it is essential to ensure that it does not bang its head or swallow its tongue when having an episode. It is possible that environmental stimuli or stress can trigger a seizure, so owners are often advised to monitor any common factors related to seizures in order to eliminate them.

Diabetes This manifests itself in canines in the same way it does in humans. A dog with this condition will require a specialist diet and regular check-ups to monitor the condition. Dachshunds are prone to diabetes but it can occur in any breed, particularly older dogs.

Arthritis Most older dogs will suffer from arthritis. Active and, conversely, heavy breeds are particularly prone to the condition, which can be painful and may seriously affect mobility. Feeding oily fish and flax oil may prevent the onset of arthritis, while physiotherapy, hydrotherapy and magnotherapy can reduce pain.

▶ Hydrotherapy can help with arthritis and recovery from injury. Here, a dog is exercising in a water treadmill.

▲ Eyes that appear cloudy can indicate cataracts, which should be treated swiftly, before they lead to loss of sight.

Bloat This is a potentially fatal condition that effects large-breed dogs, particularly those with deep chests, such as the Rhodesian Ridgeback. Bloat is brought on by a concentration of gases that forces the stomach to rotate, causing it to twist. Bloat can be caused by dogs being active too soon after eating, or eating too large an amount of food too quickly.

Hip dysplasia An abnormal positioning of the hip joint, this is commonly associated with poor breeding, and if a parent is a sufferer then it is likely that the offspring will suffer too. Dogs that suffer from hip dysplasia can be observed walking with a stilted gait and may often become lame. The condition can worsen if the dog walks frequently on a smooth, polished surface.

Elbow dysplasia Like hip dysplasia, elbow dysplasia is associated with poor breeding. It is less common than hip dysplasia but can cause equally severe pain and limitation of mobility. Large dogs are more prone to both types of dysplasia.

Cataracts These are relatively common in all breeds of dog when they reach old age but Poodles are particularly prone. They are treatable through surgery but will lead to blindness if left untreated. Looking for signs of clouding in the eye or evidence of limited sight, such as the dog acting clumsily, can help an owner identify cataracts early on.

Deafness Some breeds are prone to deafness, such as Bull Terriers and Boxers and dogs that have solid-white coats, but it can occur in any breed. Dogs can cope with deafness relatively easily but any training will require the use of exclusively visual stimuli.

Rabies This is not as common as it used to be and does not exist in the British Isles – though any dogs traveling outside the UK need to be vaccinated. It can be passed between species, and humans can catch this normally fatal disease. Symptoms include hyper-activity, aggression, excitability and paralysis in later stages. A rabid dog will rarely survive.

Breed-specific inherited conditions There are certain conditions and diseases that are more prevalent in certain breeds. Attempts to breed out such inherited diseases are being made, but the limited breeding stock that has been used in many modern breeds means that it is essential for breeders themselves to avoid using dogs with certain diseases.

General Health Problems

Dogs are prone to suffering from diet- and environment-related conditions – allergies, skin problems and parasites are relatively common among most breeds of dog. Good husbandry, grooming and diet are the best way to prevent a dog suffering unnecessarily from such problems.

Vets can advise on treatments and preventions for the various conditions that are common in dogs. Flea infestations and other parasitic infestations can be prevented with medication and good grooming. If left untreated, worms and other parasites can cause complications that will eventually lead to death if ignored. Loss of hair and rapid weight loss are signs that a dog may be carrying a parasite. Health problems can be treated by various traditional or complementary methods. Vets may prescribe a course of treatment that combines both approaches. On some occasions a vet may prescribe a special diet for a dog to get over the symptoms of an infection or illness. Certain foods, such as seaweed and flax seed, are very good at ensuring dogs remain in good and robust health.

▶ Hip displasia is most common among the larger breeds, such as Great Danes. It can be a genetic condition.

Accidents and First Aid

Being inquisitive and active animals, it is likely that every dog will have an accident at least once in its life. Prevention is always better than cure when it comes to accidents, and limiting the exposure to risk that a dog encounters in and around the home is part of responsible dog ownership.

Road Accidents

In the majority of cases dogs sustain serious trauma if hit by a motor vehicle. Head injuries and broken bones are common; crushing is also a serious risk when a dog is involved in a collision with a car. If a dog is hit by a car the most important thing to do is seek emergency veterinary assistance. Any bleeding should be stemmed by applying pressure to the wound. If it is necessary to move the dog, make sure that the head and neck are kept stable at all times.

Falls

Dogs that have fallen, either from a great height or down a flight of stairs, may sustain a variety of injuries. Head trauma, broken bones and shock are common. If a dog

◄ Dogs are adventurous animals, and sadly most will incur an injury at some time or other. Look into dog insurance cover.

► Terriers are particularly prone to suffering poisoning, if, while ratting, they catch and eat a poisoned rat.

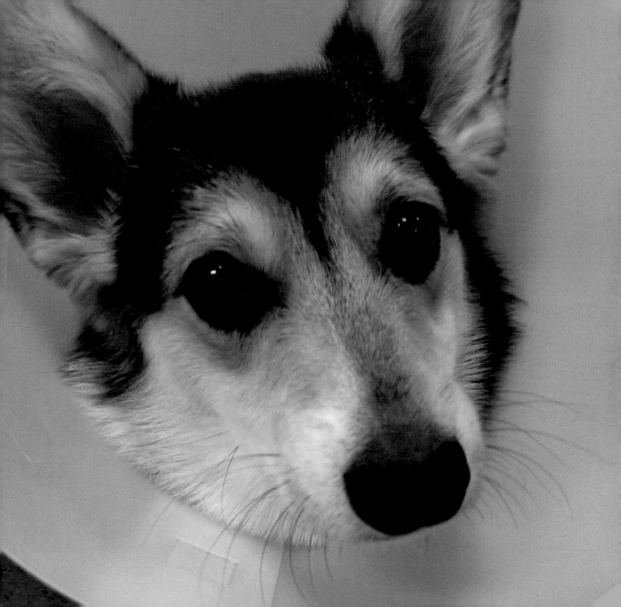

goes into shock it is important to help the dog remain calm. Keep it warm and ensure that it takes water. Stabilize any damaged limbs and seek veterinary help immediately. Preventing dogs from having access to areas where they could fall is universally more preferable than dealing with the consequences.

Burns

Burns are typically incurred on the paw pads, nose, tail and mouth. When dealing with a burn, clean the affected area and apply cold water or a damp cloth. Always see the vet in the case of a burn so that the wound can be dressed correctly. Severe burns can cause a dog to go into shock; try to ensure that the dog does not become excited and attempt to regulate body temperature using a blanket.

Poisoning

Education and prevention is essential to limit the chances of dogs ingesting harmful substances. If a dog ingests a toxin, such as anti-freeze, it may not be evident until the dog begins to become ill. If you suspect the dog has been poisoned seek veterinary assistance immediately. It is a good idea to take a sample of the poison to the vet if possible. Terriers are often poisoned if they catch a rat or mouse that has already ingested poison. Induce vomiting with salt water only on the advice of a veterinary professional.

Choking

Choking is a risk that most dogs face. Ensuring that bones are not likely to splinter and that sticks thrown are dry and solid is a necessity. If the dog begins to choke, attempt to remove the item from the airway. If this is not possible, remain calm and visit the vet. If time is limited a vet may advise that you try pumping the chest by holding the dog's head below its body and squeezing the rib cage, ensuring not to break the ribs.

▶ Many breeds of dog adore retrieving sticks, but be aware that they can pose a choking hazard.

Drowning

Cases of dogs drowning in garden ponds and pools are more common than many people realize. Depending on the amount of water taken in it may be necessary to pump the chest. Do so until the dog begins to expel the water, then always seek subsequent veterinary assistance to reduce the possibility of complications, such as pneumonia or shock.

Caring For an Elderly Dog

As sad as it is, the health of a dog will inevitably decline with old age. Taking steps to ensure that the dog is comfortable and that its quality of life is not diminished unnecessarily is essential. Simple, practical changes often make a large difference; sometimes more drastic steps are required.

Deafness and Blindness

Most dogs experience hearing or sight loss to a certain extent due to old age, but some dogs do lose all their hearing or become completely blind. This can cause certain problems but there are ways to cope with it. In the case of deafness, make changes to the layout of your home, where possible, so that the dog is able to rely more on sight. Where loss of sight is the problem, ensuring that there are no hazards in the home, such as sharp objects or open fires, limits the risk of injury to a blind dog. Dogs will adapt remarkably well to loss of sight and will come to rely on their memory to move about the home.

Mobility Issues

Some dogs struggle to remain active in old age. Keeping the dog's toys in an easy-to-reach place helps avoid injury. Dogs often do not associate their pain with movement so may flinch when hurt, but will not stop attempting to act like a young dog. In such cases, ensure that the dog does not run or jump unnecessarily.

Breeding

All dogs have a natural urge to reproduce, but as there are many dogs now in need of a home the canine population requires monitoring. Breeding should only be carried out with the intention of advancing the breed or continuing a strong and healthy bloodline. Matings should be conducted responsibly, with the welfare and health of the dogs being paramount. Special care should be taken to ensure the health of pregnant and brooding bitches, as well as the resulting litter.

Why Breed?

Breeding dogs is a huge responsibility for anyone. Only people with a sound knowledge of and passion for a particular breed should attempt it. Nothing other than dogs free from health problems and of good temperament should be used as breeding stock. Commercial breeding has a negative effect on dogs as it creates an incentive for over-breeding. The aim of breeding is to magnify and continue desirable traits in a breed.

Mating

Bringing two dogs together to mate should be done with care and consideration. Bitches only come into season approximately twice a year, while dogs are able to reproduce at any time. The process of

▶ Despite the ever-cute lure of adorable puppies, do not forget that breeding a litter is a large responsibility.

reproduction can be quite aggressive in certain cases, with bitches likely to feel discomfort when being mated. It is essential for breeders to be on hand to supervise a mating should anything go wrong. Typically, natural urges will be enough for the bitch and the dog to mate successfully.

Reproduction

Male dogs have typical mammalian reproductive organs: a penis and testicles are located at the loins. The erect penis will deliver semen from the testes into the bitch. Bitches also have typical mammalian reproductive organs.

Around twice a year a bitch will come into heat. The first phase of this cycle is called proestrous, lasting four to 15 days, where there may be discharge from thevagina that may be bloody. After this is estrous, when she is ready to be fertilized, and will give off a scent that is irresistible to male dogs. She will become sexually interested in most male dogs that she encounters. In many cases a bitch will become moody when in heat, while dogs typically become restless, distracted and aroused if they can detect the hormones that indicate a bitch's availability. Howling, whining and heavy panting are signs

that a male dog has picked up a scent froma female that is available for mating.

The Mating Process

In the wild the male will approach the female. He will signal his intent to mate in many ways, including folding his ears back and mimicking the mating movements. He

◀ There's no 'wining or dining', so either of the dogs can become distressed during mating. Here an owner comforts her bitch.

▲ This pair of dogs have 'tied': after mating the male dog dismounts and turns round, but remains inside the female for a while.

may not signal any intent and simply attempt a clumsy negotiation of the bitch, to which she may react aggressively. If amenable the bitch will typically display herself to the dog, enabling him to mount her. In some cases, however, despite being in season a bitch will not want to mate with a particular dog. If a dog attempts to mate a bitch in this scenario she may become aggressive towards him. The mating process is often forceful and can result in bites and nips being delivered from both participants.

In a successful mating the dog will mount the bitch from behind and penetrate her almost instantly. The intercourse can last from a few minutes to almost an hour or more depending on the dogs. Once the male has mated the female the two dogs will tie. This is caused by the female clasping the male while his penis is still penetrated. This is a natural instinct to prevent other dogs attempting to mate the female while she is vulnerable. Tying often causes the dogs to become distressed and aggressive, often with the dog attempting to remove himself from the bitch, which can cause pain to both dogs.

During the Pregnancy

A pregnant bitch will need some extra care. Typically she will be governed by her instincts to remain safe, but the owner should take responsibility for ensuring that she has the right diet to optimize the chances of a good pregnancy. It is also important for the owner to provide a calm and safe environment for her. The bitch will experience bodily changes during pregnancy, such as weight gain, stomach enlargement and pronounced teats.

Gestation

In order to establish whether a bitch has become pregnant the owner will take her for two pregnancy tests. The first will determine the likelihood of pregnancy and the second will confirm this. The instances of miscarriage and phantom pregnancy in dogs are quite high. It is also possible that a bitch may be traumatized during the pregnancy, which may cause her to lose the puppies. Evolution has determined that bitches unable to provide adequate care for their litter are more likely to lose the pups before they develop past the embryonic stage.

Gestation lasts between 60 and 64 days. During the pregnancy the bitch may become withdrawn and moody – this is a protective instinct. It is essential that the bitch is monitored throughout the pregnancy to ensure her health and the health of the pups.

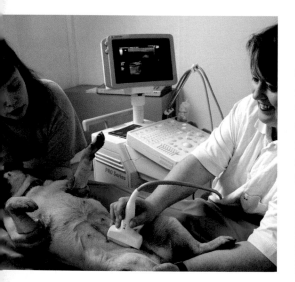

Behaviour

Behaviour during pregnancy varies from bitch to bitch. Some may remain completely normal throughout the pregnancy, showing no signs of broodiness or discomfort, while others may be overcome by maternal instincts and act in a very protective nature. It is not uncommon for pregnant bitches to practise maternal behaviour by nesting with toys. Hormonal changes within the body can lead to certain noticeable changes in temperament.

◄ Is is vital to monitor the bitch's health and that of her litter. Here a veterinary ultrasound checks the development of the litter.

► This bitch is denning – making a secure place in which to have her litter.

The Birth and After-care

Before the delivery a bitch will begin to prepare herself by denning, that is, making a den out of her bed. She will need peace, quiet and privacy in preparation. The owner or breeder should be on hand to ensure everything goes to plan and to act in case of complications, but nature usually takes its course. Some breeders prepare a whelping box for the delivery and after-care, but the bitch may prefer to find her own space – typically a secluded spot away from noise.

Litters range in size but typically are around six in number. Stillborn pups are common and it is also not rare for pups to die shortly after birth. In less common cases the mother may kill certain pups. Some believe this is linked to the bitch attempting to preserve her resources for the healthier puppies.

Delivery

During the delivery the bitch may experience pain or distress. This is quite normal and the bitch will prefer to be left to her own devices. Her temperature will increase just prior to delivery, which may cause her to pant heavily. The delivery will last anywhere between six and 12 hours, possibly longer with larger breeds.

Once the pups are born the bitch may become very protective over them, or she may appear harassed by their presence; both behaviours are normal. In some cases the pups may need special attention, so it is necessary for the breeder or owner to pay attention to any puppies that are moving less than their siblings. It is likely that the mother will need to relieve herself after giving birth and she will be keen not to soil the den.

As mentioned in the 'Puppy Care' section of the book (see pp 182–7), thorough after-care is required once delivery is complete.

▶ A one-day-old Cocker Spaniel puppy. It will be another fortnight before it can see or hear.

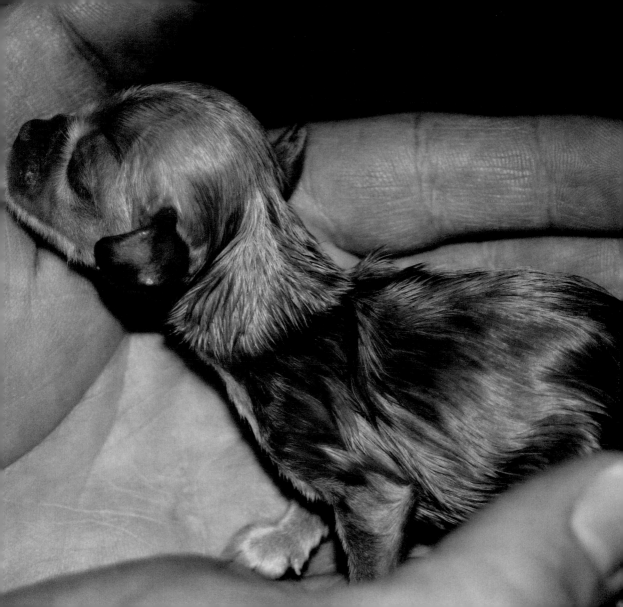

Dog Shows

Dog shows are a popular competitive pursuit for many breed enthusiasts. They are an opportunity for breeders, owners and dog lovers to meet and see lots of pure-bred dogs of differing breeds. It is also an important part of breed culture, with standards being examined and good examples of breeds being displayed for the public. Dog shows for conformation are typically open only to pure-bred or pedigree dogs, but there are conformation competitions for cross breeds and mixed breeds too.

Entering Your Dog

A dog owner may wish to enter a conformation contest in order to see how well their dog measures up to the accepted standard for its breed. Breeders that do well in conformation shows will receive acclaim and respect from their peers. Quite often fees paid to breeders for their pups or the use of their stud dogs and brood bitches increase if their animals have performed well in a conformation show.

Some people enter their dogs for fun, while others enter due to their passion for advancing and improving the breed. Competition is often heated, but in general most competitors are there for their love of the dogs.

How to Enter

In order to enter a dog into a conformation show it must be a pure-bred or pedigree. A pedigree is issued and accredited by the kennel club or equivalent of the country in which the dog was born. It lists the ancestors of the dog and any of their relevant awards and titles. A pedigree dog will have an official pedigree name, typically containing the affix of the kennel where it was bred. Each dog show is different,

so it is necessary for people to consult the guidelines of their national kennel club for information on how to enter, but typically entry involves preliminary qualification at local and regional level before competition at national or international level.

Preparing and Showing Your Dog

When showing a dog the most important thing to demonstrate is how good an example of the breed the individual dog is. Some breed standards are more specific than others, but they all offer a fairly comprehensive guide as to the size, weight, colour and general appearance of the dog. Breed standards purport to govern temperament, but this is difficult for a judge to assess during a short encounter in the show ring.

Pre-show Grooming and Preparation

A glossy, well-groomed coat is all-important for the dog to look in good health. Feeding specialist food prior to the show to improve the appearance of the coat is common. The dog should be clean and free from blemishes and marks. The teeth should be healthy and brushed, and the coat presented traditionally.

The dog should be used to being handled and demonstrated. Practising the moves that will be performed is essential, as is good socialization and an ability not to be put off by other dogs. A show judge will want to see that the dog carries itself in accordance with the breed standard and will require a competitor to walk with their dog. If the dog becomes excited or distracted it may be disqualified or marked down.

Judging

The judges are looking for conformation to type. In the instance of two dogs being too close to call physically, their gait and general demeanour in accordance to the breed standard will be taken into account. The judge will also base his or her decision on the apparent health and condition of the dog.

Useful Addresses

Care & Management

Association of Pet Behaviour Counsellors
PO Box 46 .
Worcester
WR8 9YS
UK
Tel: +44 (0)1386 751151
www.apbc.org.uk

Association of Pet Dog Trainers
PO Box 17
Kempsford
GL7 4WZ
UK
Tel: +44 (0)1285 810811
www.apdt.co.uk

Blue Cross (head office)
Shilton Road
Burford
Oxon OX18 4PF
UK
Tel: +44 (0)1993 822651
www.bluecross.org.uk

Royal College of Veterinary Surgeons
Belgravia House
62–64 Horseferry Road
London SW1P 2AF
UK
Tel: +44 (0)20 7222 2001

People's Dispensary for Sick Animals (PDSA)
Whitechapel Way, Priorslee, Telford
Shropshire
TF2 9PQ
UK
Tel: +44 (0)1952 290 999
www.pdsa.org.uk

Support Dogs

Guide Dogs for the Blind Association
Hillfields
Burghfield Common
Reading RG7 3YG
UK Tel: +44 (0)118 9835 555
www.guidedogs.org.uk

Hearing Dogs for Deaf People
Wycombe Road
Saunderton
Princes Risborough
Buckinghamshire
HP27 9NS
UK
Tel: +44 (0)1844 348 100
www.hearingdogs.org.uk

Kennel Clubs

The Kennel Club (Headquarters)
1–5 Clarges St
Piccadilly, London
W1J 8AB
UK
Tel: +44 (0)870 606 6750
www.thekennelclub.org.uk

The Kennel Club (Registrations)
4a Alton House
Gatehouse Way
Aylesbury, Bucks
HP19 8XU
UK
Tel: +44 (0)870 606 6750
www.thekennelclub.org.uk

Federation Cynologique Internationale
FCI Office
Place Albert 1er, 13B-6530
ThuinBelgique
Tel: +32 71 59 12 38
www.fci.be

Australian National Kennel Council
(check website for regional contacts)
www.ankc.org.au

New Zealand Kennel Club
Prosser St.
Private Bag 50903
Porirua 5240
New Zealand
Tel: +64 (04) 237 4489
www.nzkc.org.nz

Kennel Union of Southern Africa
PO Box 2659
Cape Town 8000
South Africa
Tel: +27 21 423 9027
www.kusa.co.za

Japan Kennel Club
1–5 Kanda Suda-chochiyoda-ku
Tokyo 101-8552
Japan
Tel: +81 3 32 511 651
www.jkc.or.jp

American Kennel Club
260 Madison Ave.
New York City
NY 10016
USA
Tel: +1 919 233 9767
www.akc.org

United Kennel Club
100 E Kilgore Rd
KalamazooMI 49002-5584
USA
Tel: +1 269 343 9020
www.ukcdogs.com

The Canadian Kennel Club
89 Skyway Ave, Suite 100
Etobicoke, Ontario
M0W 6R4
Canada
Tel: +1 416 675 5511
www.ckc.ca

Welfare Organisations

Battersea Dogs Home
4 Battersea Park Road
London SW8 4AA
UK
Tel: +44 (0)207 622 3626
www.battersea.org.uk

Dogs Trust
17 Wakley St
London EC1V 7RQ
UK
Tel: +44 (0)20 7837 0006
www.dogstrust.org.uk

Department for Environment,
Food & Rural Affairs
Nobel House
17 Smith Square
London SW1P 3JR
UK
Tel: +44 (0)8459 556000
www.defra.gov.uk

Royal Society for the Prevention of
Cruelty to Animals
RSPCA Enquiries Service
Wilberforce Way
Southwater Horsham
West Sussex
RH13 9RS
UK
Tel: +44 (0)300 1423 999
www.rspca.org.uk

Scottish Society for the Prevention
of Cruelty to Animals
Braehead Mains 603 Queensferry Rd
Edinburgh EH4 6EA
Scotland
UK
Tel: +44 (0)131 339 0222
www.scottishspca.org

Irish Society for the Prevention
of Cruelty to Animals
National Animal Centre
Derryglogher Lodge
Keenagh County
Longford
Ireland
Tel: +353 043 250 35
www.ispca.ie

RSPCA Australia Inc
PO Box 265
Deakin West ACT 2600
Australia
Tel: +61 (02) 6282 8300
www.rspca.org.au

Royal New Zealand Society
for the Prevention of Cruelty
to Animals
PO Box 15349
New Lynn Auckland
New Zealand
Tel: +64 (09) 827 6094
www.rnzspca.org.nz

American Society for the
Prevention of Cruelty to
Animals (ASPCA)
424 E 92nd St
New York
NY 10128-6804
USA
Tel: +1 212 876 7700
www.aspca.org

Humane Society of the
United States HSUS
Headquarters 2100 L St
NW Washington DCDC 20037
USA
Tel: +1 202 452 1100
www.humanesociety.org

The Animal Welfare Foundation
of Canada
Suite 616, 410 Bank St
Ottawa, Ontario
K2P 1Y8
Canada
Email: info@awfc.cawww.awfc.ca

Canadian Federation of
Humane Societies
102-30 Concourse Gate
Ottawa
Ontario K2E 7V7
Canada
Tel: +1 888 678 CFHS
www.cfhs.ca

Further Reading

Abrantes, Roger *The Evolution of Canine Social Behaviour*, Dogwise Publishing (Washington, USA), 2003

Acker, Randy; Fergus, Jim; Smith, Christopher, *Dog First Aid: Emergency Care for the Hunting, Working, and Outdoor Dog (A Field Guide)*, Wilderness Adventure Press (Michigan, USA), 1994

Alderton, David, *Top to Tail: The 360 Degrees Guide to Picking Your Perfect Pet*, David & Charles (Devon, UK), 2004

American Kennel Club, *The Complete Dog Book: 20th Edition*, Ballantine Books (New York City, USA), 2006

American Rescue Dog Association, *Search and Rescue Dogs: Training Methods*, Prentice-Hall (London, UK), 1991

Atkinson, Eleanor, *Greyfriars Bobby*, Puffin Classics (London, UK), 1995

Bailey, Gwen, *Choosing the Right Dog For You: Profiles of Over 200 Dog Breeds*, Hamlyn (London, UK), 2004

Becker, Marty; Spadafori, Gina, *Why Do Dogs Drink Out of the Toilet?: 101 of the Most Perplexing Questions Answered about Canine Conundrums, Medical Mysteries & Befuddling Behaviors*, Health Communications (Florida, USA), 2006

Chance, Paul, *Learning and Behavior*, Wadsworth Publishing Co. Inc. (Connecticut), 2002

Fennel, Jan, *The Seven Ages of Man's Best Friend: A Comprehensive Guide to Caring For Your Dog Through All the Stages of Life*, Collins (London, UK), 2007

Fergus, Charles, *Gun Dog Breeds: A Guide to Spaniels, Retrievers and Pointing Dogs*, The Lyons Press (Connecticut, USA), 2003

Finder Harris, Beth J., *Breeding a Litter: The Complete Book of Prenatal and Postnatal Care*, John Wiley & Sons (New Jersey, USA), 1993

Goody, Peter C., *Dog Anatomy: A Pictorial Approach to Canine Structure*, J.A. Allen & Co. Ltd (California, USA), 1999

Grogan, John, *Marley & Me: Life and Love with the World's Worst Dog*, William Morrow (New York City, USA), 2006

Hynes, Bruce, *The Noble Newfoundland Dog: A History in Stories, Legends, and the Occasional Tall Tale*, Nimbus Publishing (Nova Scotia, Canada), 2005

Knight, Eric *Lassie Come Home*, Holt, Rinehart and Winston (Austin, Texas, USA), 1940

Lane, Dick; Ewart, Neil, *A-Z of Dog Diseases and Common Health Problems*, Ringpress Books Ltd (Gloucestershire, UK), 1996

Lane, Marion S., *The Humane Society of the United States Complete Guide to Dog Care: Everything You Need to Know to Keep Your Dog Healthy and Happy*, Little, Brown and Company (London, UK), 2001

London, Jack, *The Call of the Wild*, Aladdin Classics (Ontario & New Jersey, USA; London, UK), 2003

Pryor, Karen, *Don't Shoot the Dog!: The New Art of Teaching and Training*, Ringpress Books Ltd (Gloucestershire, UK), 2002

Rice, Dan, *Small Dog Breeds*, Barron's Educational Series (New York, USA), 2002

Saunders, Marshall, *Beautiful Joe: A Dog's Own Story*, Book Jungle (Illinois, USA), 2006

Secord, William, *Dog Painting 1840–1940: A Social History of the Dog in Art*, Antique Collectors' Club Ltd (Suffolk, UK), 1999

Serpell, James, *The Domestic Dog: Its Evolution, Behaviour and Interactions with People*, Cambridge University Press (Cambridge, UK), 1995

Stilwell, Victoria, *It's Me or the Dog: How to Have the Perfect Pet*, Collins (London, UK), 2005

Stone, Ben; Stone, Peal, *The Stone Guide to Dog Grooming for All Breeds*, John Wiley & Sons (New Jersey, USA), 1981

Tanner, Michael, *The Legend of Mick the Miller*, Highdown (London, UK), 2004

Taylor, David, *The British Veterinary Association Guide to Dog Care*, Dorling Kindersley Publishers Ltd (London, UK), 1989

Thomson, Laura, *The Dogs: A Personal History of Greyhound Racing*, High Stakes Publishing (Harpenden, UK), 2003

Thurston, Mary Elizabeth, *The Lost History of the Canine Race: Our 15,000-Year Love Affair With Dogs*, Andrews Mcmeel Publishing (New Jersey, USA), 2006

Glossary

Action The way in which a dog runs or moves when working. This term is normally applied when dogs are being judged at work or in conformation.

Athletic Describes the look or carriage of a lean, strong dog. Typically sight hounds and working breeds are described as athletic.

Basset A type of dog originating in France, typified by short legs. Examples are Basset Hound, Grand Basset Griffin Vendeen and Basset Fauve de Bretagne.

Belton White and coloured hairs growing together to give the appearance of other colours, such as lemon.

Blaze White stripe separating other colours, typical of tricolour colouration, as exemplified by the Bernese Mountain Dog.

Bite The position in which a dog's teeth naturally come to rest.

Bob tail A naturally short tail.

Bold Describes the typical character of an outgoing, confident breed. Terrier breeds can often be described as bold.

Boisterous Describes the typical character of a curious and fearless dog breed. Certain terrier breeds and some pointer breeds can be described as boisterous.

Bracco Italian term for pointer type.

Braque French term for pointer type.

Breed Name used to identify dogs of a distinct type and bloodline. Labrador Retriever, Doberman or English Springer Spaniel are all names of breeds.

Breed, to The process by which owners intentionally encourage two dogs to mate under controlled conditions in order to create offspring of the same breed.

Breed standard Document outlining parameters of size, colour and appearance of a dog breed.

Breed true, to The process by which a new breed begins to display uniformity of physical characteristics.

Breeding stock Individual dogs that are used for mating in order to generate offspring of a certain breed.

Brindle A striped coat pattern.

Canid Taxonomical reference to members of the dog family, including wolves, dogs and foxes.

Carriage The identifiable way in which a dog holds its head, moves its legs and stands.

Coat The fur of a dog in its entirety, used when describing length, texture and colour.

Conformation A type of competition in which an individual dog is judged on its closeness to its type.

Crop Cosmetic procedure performed on a dog's ears to make them stand on end.

Cur Generic American term for a dog of unidentifiable heritage, commonly used to describe semi-wild dogs.

Demeanour Describes the typical way in which a dog interacts with humans and other dogs presuming there are no mitigating behavioural or environmental factors.

Dewclaw Fifth digit found at the back of the pastern on some breeds. Depending on breed and circumstances this is often removed by a vet.

Dewlap Growth of fur below the jaw, particularly pronounced in certain breeds, notably Mastiff types.

Dock To shorten the length of a dog's tail by removing a portion of it, normally performed by a vet for cosmetic or practical working reasons. This procedure is illegal in the UK.

Dominant Descriptive of either an individual dog or breed that is likely to assert superiority over other dogs and people. Normally describes an individual member of a litter or pack.

Down breed, to To deliberately decrease the standard size of a breed by using smaller breeds or smaller examples of the same breed in order to create a smaller type.

Drive Instinctive desire or action found in all dogs. Includes play drive, hunt drive and defence drive.

Drop Describes long, pendulous ears. Scent Hounds typically have drop ears.

Erect Describes ears that naturally stand on top of the head.

Even temper An even-tempered breed is unlikely to respond excitedly or unpredictably to the majority of standard stimuli.

Family Normally refers to a collection of breeds descended from the same type. For example, 'Northern European Spitz Family'.

Ferocious Describes a dog that is typically adept at fighting, hunting or protecting.

Gait The distinctive manner in which a dog mobilizes or moves. This can aid identification of ancestry in crossbreeds, or mixed breeds, of undetermined ancestry.

Group A group, or breed group, is the means of categorizing breeds by using criteria such as function or form.

Guardian Describes the natural attributes or personality of a breed established to protect people or livestock.

Gun shy Describes the tendency of some dogs to exhibit fear in the proximity of gun fire, particularly relevant to sporting and gun-dog breeds.

Hardy Describes the physical and behavioural nature of a dog bred to demonstrate a high tolerance for cold, exhaustion, discomfort or solitude.

Herding Descriptive of dogs bred to control the movement of livestock.

Jowls Folds of skin about the mouth and jaw, particularly pronounced in Molosser-type dogs.

Mask Used to describe the face of a dog or breed when the face is a different colour, normally black, compared to the rest of the body.

Merle Describes a coat colouration that displays a marbled effect of dark fur against lighter fur.

Mixed breed A dog with more than two breeds in its ancestry. For example, the offspring of two crossbreeds.

Molosser Describes a type of heavy, powerfully built dog with a large head that is thought to descend from the ancient Molossus.

Muzzle The part of a dog's face where a muzzle would be placed. It is used as a term to describe the nature of the face, for example 'wide muzzle'.

Non-pedigree A dog that does not have a pedigree to confirm its ancestry. Crossbreeds and mixed breeds are non-pedigree dogs.

Outcross, to To introduce the blood of another breed or variation in order for a breed to acquire certain attributes. This is often done when new breeds are being established or as a means to strengthen the gene pool of an existing breed.

Pastoral A description of a dog's instincts or the name of a breed group as governed by a kennel club. It is analogous with the term 'herding'.

Pedigree A document that confirms and details the genetic ancestry of a dog. It is also a term used to denote pure breeding.

Pointer A type of gun dog or sporting breed that is trained to indicate the location of game or prey to its master by fixing itself into a point position.

Recognized For a breed to be recognized, a kennel club or similar authority must agree to the standard for that breed. There are lots of breeds that are recognized in certain parts of the world and not in others.

Retriever A type of gun-dog breed that was established to be soft of mouth, in order to return game and prey carefully to its master.

Rustic Term used to describe a breed of dog that typically displays characteristics that are suitable for outdoor living and survival in particularly harsh or challenging environments such as hills. 'Rustic' is a general and intangible term that is used to refer to the overall appearance and temperament of a dog or breed.

Sable A type of coat colouration defined by black-tipped hairs on a paler background.

Saddle An area of a dog's coat that is of different colour to the main colour. The saddle is in the area near the bottom of the back where a saddle would be fitted to a horse.

Setter A type of gun dog that is bred and trained to indicate the location of game, particularly birds.

Show-bred A show-bred dog is a variation of a breed that is distinct from its counterpart working variety because it was bred to conform to the breed standard rather than for its working ability. Show-bred dogs can differ quite a lot from work-bred versions of the same breed the Cocker Spaniel is a good example of this.

Spitz A family of dogs or type of breed that includes the Samoyed, Pomeranian and Finnish Spitz. The breeds typically have thick coats, erect ears and alert facial expressions.

Standardized A breed becomes standardized when each litter displays a uniform set of characteristics and attributes. The offspring of standardized breeds are of predictable appearance.

Temperament A general means of describing the likely reactions of an individual dog or breed to certain stimuli. For example, a dog that is protective in its temperament may be more likely to respond suspiciously to the presence of a stranger in its home. Suitability of temperament is an important factor to consider when choosing your dog.

Terrier A type of dog breed that is descended from dogs that were bred to catch vermin. More modern terrier breeds have been established as companion and guarding breeds.

Terrier instinct Refers to stimulation by small moving animals and, in some cases, objects. It describes an action that is closely associated with terrier breeds but can apply to certain other dogs.

Toy breed A breed that was bred specifically to provide companionship. Certain toy breeds started life as working breeds but have adapted to domestic companionship. Toy breeds are typically small.

Tricolour A type of coat colouration that has three colours. Typically tricolour comes in black, white and tan.

Type Used in conjunction with another word, such as 'Mastiff' or 'Spitz', to describe the appearance of an individual dog or breed.

Watchdog A breed or individual dog that is required to alert its owner to the presence of potential intruders. It is also used to distinguish between guard dogs, which are watchdogs that are also required to deal with intruders, and dogs that are incapable of dealing with an intruder except for signalling their presence.

Working Describes any breed that is or was used predominantly to fulfil a function other than companionship.

Index